Decolonization and Independence Movements: Shaping the Modern World

Oswald D. B.

Published by Oswald, 2024.

DECOLONIZATION AND INDEPENDENCE MOVEMENTS: SHAPING THE MODERN WORLD

First edition. September 6, 2024.

Copyright © 2024 Oswald D. B..

ISBN: 979-8227129581

Written by Oswald D. B..

Table of Contents

Introduction: A New Dawn of Freedom

Decolonization, a powerful movement of the 20th century, marked the end of centuries-long imperial domination by European powers over vast territories in Asia, Africa, and the Caribbean. This seismic shift in global power dynamics began in the aftermath of World War II and unfolded over several decades, fundamentally altering the political, social, and economic landscapes of the world. As the old colonial empires crumbled, newly independent nations emerged, forging their paths toward self-determination, sovereignty, and identity. This book, **"Decolonization and Independence Movements,"** delves deep into these transformative struggles, examining the forces that drove them, the challenges faced by the newly sovereign states, and their enduring impact on global politics today.

The story of decolonization is not merely a narrative of political change; it is a tale of resilience, courage, and the unyielding human spirit in the face of oppression. The desire for freedom and self-rule ignited a spark that spread across continents, galvanizing people from different backgrounds to fight against colonial domination. This movement was not uniform; it manifested differently across regions, reflecting the unique historical, cultural, and geopolitical contexts of each area. Yet, at its core, decolonization was a universal struggle for justice, equality, and the right to self-determination.

Global Context: The Road to Decolonization

The path to decolonization was shaped by a complex interplay of global events and forces. The two World Wars, in particular, played a crucial role in accelerating the decline of colonial empires. World War I exposed the vulnerabilities of European powers and planted the seeds of discontent among colonial subjects, many of whom fought alongside their colonizers in distant battlefields, only to return to the harsh realities of subjugation. The interwar period saw the rise of nationalist movements, as intellectuals, leaders, and ordinary people began to demand greater autonomy and rights.

World War II further weakened European colonial powers, both economically and politically. The war had drained their resources, and rebuilding war-torn economies became a priority. Additionally, the ideological struggle against fascism and the fight for democracy and human rights during the war years created a powerful contradiction: how could colonial powers justify their subjugation of other peoples while championing freedom and democracy? This moral dilemma was not lost on the colonized, who increasingly viewed their colonial masters as hypocritical and oppressive.

The post-war period also witnessed the emergence of the United States and the Soviet Union as superpowers, each with its vision of the world order. Both powers, for their strategic reasons, supported decolonization efforts, albeit in different ways. The United States, while itself grappling with racial segregation, advocated for self-determination in principle, partly to expand its influence in newly independent nations. The Soviet Union, on the other hand, saw an opportunity to spread its ideology by supporting anti-colonial movements, viewing them as allies in the global struggle against Western imperialism.

Rise of Nationalism in Asia, Africa, and the Caribbean

Nationalism emerged as a potent force driving the decolonization process. In Asia, countries like India, Indonesia, and Vietnam were at the forefront of the independence movements. India's struggle against British colonial rule, led by figures like Mahatma Gandhi and Jawaharlal Nehru, became a symbol of nonviolent resistance and inspired other movements worldwide. Similarly, in Indonesia and

Vietnam, nationalist leaders like Sukarno and Ho Chi Minh mobilized mass movements to challenge Dutch and French colonial powers, respectively.

In Africa, the push for independence gained momentum in the post-war era, driven by both urban intellectuals and rural populations. Leaders like Kwame Nkrumah in Ghana and Jomo Kenyatta in Kenya emerged as charismatic voices for freedom, advocating for Pan-Africanism and the unification of African states against colonialism. These movements were often met with fierce resistance from colonial powers, leading to prolonged struggles and, in some cases, violent conflicts.

The Caribbean region, too, saw a wave of independence movements. Here, the quest for freedom was influenced by a complex mix of colonial legacies, economic dependencies, and cultural identities. The dissolution of the West Indies Federation and the subsequent independence of Jamaica, Trinidad and Tobago, and other Caribbean nations marked a significant chapter in the decolonization process.

Key Themes of the Book

This book explores several key themes central to understanding the decolonization process and its impact on the modern world:

- **Struggles for Self-Determination:** At the heart of decolonization was the struggle for self-determination—the right of a people to decide their political status and pursue their economic, social, and cultural development. This theme will be explored through the lens of various independence movements, examining how different countries and regions fought for and achieved their freedom.
- **Impact on Global Politics:** The decolonization wave reshaped global politics, leading to the emergence of newly

independent states and the reconfiguration of international relations. The book will analyze how decolonization influenced Cold War dynamics, the formation of the Non-Aligned Movement, and the evolving nature of global diplomacy.

- **Legacies of Colonialism:** Decolonization did not erase the deep scars left by centuries of colonial rule. The book will delve into the enduring legacies of colonialism, including economic dependency, ethnic divisions, and political instability, and how these challenges continue to shape postcolonial states today.

- **Cultural Reawakening and Identity**: The quest for independence was not just a political struggle but also a cultural one. Decolonization sparked a reawakening of indigenous cultures, languages, and identities suppressed during colonial rule. The book will explore this cultural renaissance and its role in shaping postcolonial identities.

- **Economic Independence and Development Challenges:** Gaining political independence was only the first step; achieving economic independence proved to be an even greater challenge for many newly sovereign states. The book will examine the economic strategies adopted by these nations, the role of international organizations, and the ongoing struggles for economic justice and development.

- **Conflicts and Continuity:** Decolonization often led to new conflicts, both internal and external, as newly independent states grappled with the legacies of colonial borders, ethnic tensions, and political rivalries. The book will discuss these conflicts and the ongoing quest for stability and peace in postcolonial regions.

Setting the Stage: What to Expect in the Following Chapters

In the chapters that follow, we will embark on a journey across continents and decades, exploring the diverse paths to independence taken by countries in Asia, Africa, and the Caribbean. Each chapter will provide a detailed examination of specific independence movements, highlighting the unique contexts, challenges, and achievements of these struggles. From the nonviolent resistance led by Gandhi in India to the armed liberation struggles in Algeria and Vietnam, from the cultural renaissance in postcolonial Africa to the economic challenges faced by newly independent states, this book will offer a comprehensive overview of the decolonization era.

Through vivid narratives and scholarly analysis, we aim to provide readers with a deeper understanding of how these independence movements have shaped the modern world. The stories of decolonization are not just historical accounts; they are lessons in resilience, justice, and the enduring quest for freedom and self-determination. As we navigate through these complex and often turbulent histories, we will also reflect on the contemporary relevance of these struggles and what they can teach us about today's global challenges.

Why This Book Matters

Understanding the history of decolonization is crucial for anyone interested in global politics, international relations, or the ongoing quest for justice and equality. The impact of these independence movements extends far beyond the borders of the countries directly involved; they have reshaped the entire global order, influencing everything from economic policies to cultural identities and international relations.

By exploring the decolonization process in detail, this book seeks to illuminate the complex dynamics that have shaped our world and continue to influence it today. It is a call to recognize the interconnectedness of our histories and the shared responsibility to learn from them to build a more just and equitable future.

Join us on this journey through history, as we explore the powerful stories of decolonization and the enduring quest for freedom and justice that continues to inspire and challenge us today.

Part 1: The Rise of Nationalism in Asia

Chapter 1: India's Struggle for Independence

Background of British Colonial Rule in India

India's struggle for independence is a profound story of resilience, determination, and the quest for freedom from colonial rule. The British colonial presence in India began in the early 17th century with the establishment of the British East India Company, which initially focused on trade but gradually extended its control over vast territories. By the mid-19th century, after the revolt of 1857, also known as the First War of Indian Independence or the Sepoy Mutiny, the British Crown assumed direct control over India, marking the beginning of the British Raj. The Raj brought with it a system of governance that entrenched British economic, political, and cultural dominance over the Indian subcontinent.

During this period, India was subjected to exploitative economic policies, which led to widespread poverty and famine. The British dismantled India's traditional industries and imposed heavy taxes on agricultural products, forcing many farmers into debt and landlessness. Culturally, the British colonialists sought to impose their values and systems, undermining indigenous traditions and social structures. This period also saw the rise of an educated Indian middle class, who began to question British rule and advocate for political rights and reforms.

Early Resistance Movements and the Rise of Nationalism

The seeds of India's independence movement were sown in the late 19th century with the rise of Indian nationalism. The early resistance movements were characterized by both moderate and radical elements. The formation of the Indian National Congress (INC) in 1885 marked a significant step in India's struggle for freedom. Initially, the Congress sought greater representation for Indians in government and more political rights through constitutional means. However, by the turn of the century, more radical voices within the movement, such as Bal Gangadhar Tilak, Lala Lajpat Rai, and Bipin Chandra Pal, began advocating for self-rule and complete independence from British rule.

The partition of Bengal in 1905 by Lord Curzon, the then Viceroy of India, sparked widespread protests and mass mobilizations. This event is often regarded as a turning point in the Indian independence movement, as it galvanized public opinion against British rule and led to the Swadeshi Movement, which encouraged Indians to boycott British goods and promote indigenous industries. This period also saw the rise of revolutionary activities and armed resistance by groups like the Ghadar Party and the Hindustan Socialist Republican Association, who believed in direct action and armed struggle to overthrow British rule.

The Emergence of Mahatma Gandhi and the Indian National Congress

The Indian independence movement entered a new phase with the arrival of Mohandas Karamchand Gandhi, popularly known as Mahatma Gandhi, from South Africa in 1915. Gandhi brought with him the philosophy of nonviolent resistance, or Satyagraha, which he had developed and successfully employed in South Africa against racial discrimination. He believed that nonviolence was not only a moral imperative but also a practical strategy for achieving political goals. Gandhi's emphasis on nonviolent civil disobedience, truth, and non-cooperation with the colonial regime resonated with millions of Indians and became the cornerstone of the independence movement.

Under Gandhi's leadership, the Indian National Congress transformed from a moderate political organization into a mass movement that sought to mobilize all sections of Indian society. Gandhi's call for non-cooperation in 1920, in response to the Jallianwala Bagh massacre and the Rowlatt Act, marked the beginning of a new era of mass mobilization. The movement urged Indians to boycott British goods, institutions, and services and to resign from government jobs. The non-cooperation movement witnessed widespread participation from across the country, from urban elites to rural peasants. Although the movement was suspended in 1922 following the Chauri Chaura incident, it demonstrated the potential of nonviolent resistance to challenge British authority.

Gandhi's Philosophy of Nonviolent Resistance (Satyagraha)

Gandhi's philosophy of Satyagraha was rooted in the belief that nonviolence was a more powerful force than violence. He argued that true resistance to oppression could only be achieved through nonviolent means, which he believed had a transformative power to appeal to the conscience of the oppressor. Satyagraha was not passive resistance but an active form of civil disobedience that required great discipline, courage, and moral conviction. Gandhi believed that Satyagraha would not only lead to political independence but also promote social and spiritual regeneration in India.

Gandhi's philosophy was put to the test during the Salt March of 1930, one of the most iconic events in the history of India's independence struggle. In response to the British monopoly on salt production and the salt tax, Gandhi led a 240-mile march from Sabarmati Ashram to the coastal village of Dandi, where he symbolically broke the salt law by making salt from seawater. The Salt March galvanized the nation, sparking widespread acts of civil disobedience across India. Thousands of Indians participated in the campaign, openly defying British laws and facing arrest and imprisonment. The Salt March was a pivotal moment in the independence movement, demonstrating the power of nonviolent resistance and drawing international attention to India's struggle for freedom.

Key Events: The Salt March and the Quit India Movement

The Salt March was followed by a period of intense political activity, negotiations, and further campaigns. The 1930s saw the rise of new political forces, including the Muslim League, which began to demand greater representation for Muslims in any future government. Despite internal divisions, the Indian National Congress continued to advocate for complete independence from British rule.

The outbreak of World War II in 1939 marked another critical juncture in India's independence struggle. The British decision to involve India in the war without consulting Indian leaders led to widespread anger and protests. In response, the Congress launched the Quit India Movement in August 1942, demanding an end to British rule. Gandhi's call to "Do or Die" resonated with millions, leading to a massive uprising across the country. The British responded with a brutal crackdown, arresting thousands of leaders, including Gandhi, Nehru, and Patel, and suppressing the movement with force. Despite the repression, the Quit India Movement marked the final push towards independence, demonstrating the unwavering resolve of the Indian people to achieve freedom.

World War II and the Road to Independence

World War II significantly weakened the British Empire, both economically and politically. The war drained British resources and exposed the limitations of British power. At the same time, it heightened the demands for independence across the colonies. In India, the war years saw a significant rise in nationalist sentiment, with the Indian National Army (INA), led by Subhas Chandra Bose, fighting alongside the Axis powers to liberate India from British rule. Although the INA ultimately failed militarily, it played a crucial role in inspiring the Indian people and demoralizing the British authorities.

The end of World War II brought a renewed push for independence. The British government, facing mounting pressure both at home and abroad, recognized the inevitability of Indian independence. In 1945, the Labour Party, which was more sympathetic to Indian aspirations, came to power in Britain. The new government initiated negotiations with Indian leaders to transfer power and grant independence. However, deep divisions between the Congress and the

Muslim League, led by Muhammad Ali Jinnah, led to a stalemate. Jinnah's demand for a separate Muslim state, Pakistan, became a major point of contention, and communal tensions escalated across India.

The Partition of India and Pakistan in 1947

The British decision to partition India and create two independent dominions—India and Pakistan—was announced on June 3, 1947. The partition plan, which was seen as a last resort to prevent civil war, was implemented hastily, leading to one of the largest mass migrations in human history. As millions of Hindus, Muslims, and Sikhs crossed borders to join their respective countries, communal violence erupted, resulting in the deaths of hundreds of thousands of people and leaving millions displaced. The partition of India remains one of the most traumatic and contested episodes in the history of the Indian subcontinent.

On August 15, 1947, India gained independence, marking the end of nearly 200 years of British colonial rule. While independence was celebrated with joy and hope, it was also marred by the violence and suffering caused by partition. The creation of Pakistan, initially as a two-winged country (West Pakistan and East Pakistan), and the subsequent conflicts between India and Pakistan set the stage for ongoing geopolitical tensions in South Asia.

Immediate Impact on India and the Global Decolonization Movement

The independence of India had a profound impact both domestically and globally. Domestically, India faced the daunting task of nation-building, with challenges ranging from integrating princely states, addressing communal violence, and rebuilding a war-torn economy. The newly formed government, led by Prime Minister Jawaharlal Nehru, embarked on a path of democratic governance, economic planning, and social reform, aiming to lay the foundations for a modern, secular, and democratic state.

Globally, India's independence was a catalyst for decolonization across Asia, Africa, and beyond. It inspired other colonies to seek independence, providing a model for peaceful resistance and mass mobilization. The Indian experience underscored the moral and political contradictions of colonialism, leading to a reevaluation of colonial policies by European powers. India also played a leading role in the formation of the Non-Aligned Movement, advocating for a third path in the Cold War era that emphasized sovereignty, development, and peace.

India's struggle for independence is a powerful story of resilience, courage, and the quest for freedom. It is a story that continues to inspire movements for justice and equality around the world. The journey from colonial subjugation to independence was fraught with challenges, but it also demonstrated the strength and determination of a people united in their pursuit of self-determination. The lessons learned from India's experience remain relevant today as nations continue to grapple with the legacies of colonialism and the challenges of building inclusive, just, and democratic societies.

Chapter 2: The Independence Movements in Southeast Asia

Introduction: Southeast Asia on the Brink of Change

Southeast Asia, a region rich in cultural diversity and strategic significance, became a central stage for decolonization in the mid-20th century. The struggle for independence in this region was shaped by a complex interplay of local nationalist movements, colonial legacies, and global geopolitical shifts. The Japanese occupation during World War II played a pivotal role in weakening the hold of European colonial powers and sowing the seeds of independence among local populations. This chapter explores the independence movements in Southeast Asia, focusing on Indonesia's struggle against Dutch colonial rule and Vietnam's fight against French colonialism, while highlighting the significant contributions of key figures like Sukarno and Ho Chi Minh. We will also examine the importance of the Bandung

Conference in 1955 and the formation of the Non-Aligned Movement, which marked a turning point in the region's political landscape.

Japanese Occupation and Its Impact on Colonial Powers

World War II had a profound impact on Southeast Asia, particularly through the Japanese occupation from 1941 to 1945. The Japanese imperial forces swept through the region, rapidly dismantling the colonial administrations of the British, Dutch, and French. In many Southeast Asian countries, the Japanese presented themselves as liberators, promising to free the region from Western colonial rule. While their primary objective was to expand Japan's imperial control, the Japanese occupation unintentionally fostered anti-colonial sentiments and nationalist movements.

The Japanese occupation disrupted the status quo, dismantling colonial structures and weakening the European powers' grip on the region. In countries like Indonesia and Vietnam, the Japanese provided limited support to local nationalist movements, hoping to use them as instruments to further their own strategic goals. However, this short-term support inadvertently empowered nationalist leaders, who later became pivotal figures in their countries' struggles for independence.

The end of World War II left a power vacuum in Southeast Asia, as Japan's defeat led to the withdrawal of its forces. The returning colonial powers faced a radically changed political landscape, with rising nationalist movements demanding independence. The Japanese occupation had exposed the vulnerability of the European colonial powers and had provided an opening for local leaders to assert their right to self-determination.

Indonesia's Struggle for Independence Against the Dutch

Indonesia's path to independence was marked by a determined struggle against Dutch colonial rule, which had controlled the archipelago for over three centuries. The Indonesian independence movement gained momentum during the Japanese occupation, which weakened Dutch authority and allowed nationalist leaders to organize and mobilize support. Sukarno and Mohammad Hatta emerged as the key figures in the fight for Indonesian independence.

On August 17, 1945, just days after Japan's surrender, Sukarno and Hatta proclaimed Indonesia's independence, marking the beginning of a four-year armed struggle against the Dutch, who sought to reestablish control over their former colony. This period, known as the Indonesian National Revolution, was characterized by fierce fighting, diplomacy, and mass mobilization. The newly formed Indonesian National Army (Tentara Nasional Indonesia, or TNI), consisting of former Japanese-trained militias and local fighters, waged a guerrilla war against the returning Dutch forces.

The international context played a crucial role in Indonesia's independence struggle. The United States and the Soviet Union, emerging as superpowers after World War II, pressured the Dutch to negotiate with the Indonesian nationalists. The Indonesian cause also garnered widespread sympathy among other Asian and African countries, many of which were themselves fighting against colonial rule. The United Nations intervened, leading to a series of negotiations between the Dutch and the Indonesian republic. The Linggadjati Agreement of 1947 and the Renville Agreement of 1948, however, failed to resolve the conflict, resulting in continued hostilities.

The situation reached a turning point in December 1948, when the Dutch launched a military offensive, capturing Yogyakarta, the temporary capital of the Indonesian Republic, and imprisoning Sukarno and other leaders. However, this move backfired, as it galvanized international condemnation and increased domestic support for the independence cause. Under mounting global pressure, particularly from the United States, which threatened to cut off Marshall Plan aid to the Netherlands, the Dutch were forced to negotiate a settlement.

On December 27, 1949, the Dutch formally transferred sovereignty to the United States of Indonesia, marking the end of colonial rule. However, the process of nation-building in Indonesia was far from over, as the new nation faced challenges of political instability, regional separatism, and economic reconstruction.

Vietnam's Fight for Independence Against the French

Vietnam's struggle for independence against French colonial rule was a defining moment in the decolonization of Southeast Asia. The Vietnamese independence movement, led by the Viet Minh under the leadership of Ho Chi Minh, emerged as a formidable force during World War II. The Japanese occupation of Vietnam weakened French control, allowing the Viet Minh to consolidate power in the northern regions.

On September 2, 1945, Ho Chi Minh declared the independence of the Democratic Republic of Vietnam (DRV) in Hanoi, citing the American Declaration of Independence and the French Revolution as inspirations. However, France, determined to restore its colonial empire, refused to recognize Vietnamese independence and launched a military campaign to reassert control over the region.

The First Indochina War, which lasted from 1946 to 1954, was a brutal conflict marked by guerrilla warfare, conventional battles, and significant civilian casualties. The Viet Minh, with support from China and the Soviet Union, waged a relentless struggle against the French forces, employing guerrilla tactics and building support among the rural population. The French, despite their superior military capabilities, found themselves bogged down in a protracted and costly conflict.

The turning point in the war came in 1954 at the Battle of Dien Bien Phu, where the Viet Minh, led by General Vo Nguyen Giap, decisively defeated the French forces. The French defeat at Dien Bien Phu marked the end of French colonial ambitions in Indochina and set the stage for the Geneva Conference, where an agreement was reached to temporarily divide Vietnam at the 17th parallel, with the North under the control of the DRV and the South under a pro-Western regime. This division, however, laid the groundwork for future conflict, eventually leading to the Vietnam War.

The Bandung Conference and the Formation of the Non-Aligned Movement

The Bandung Conference, held in April 1955 in Bandung, Indonesia, was a significant milestone in the decolonization movement in Southeast Asia and beyond. The conference brought together representatives from 29 Asian and African countries, many of which had recently gained independence or were in the process of doing so. The leaders of these nations, including Sukarno, Nehru, Nasser, and Zhou Enlai, convened to discuss mutual concerns, promote economic and cultural cooperation, and assert their right to self-determination.

The Bandung Conference marked the first major international gathering of postcolonial nations and laid the foundation for the Non-Aligned Movement (NAM), which would be formally established in 1961. The NAM sought to provide an alternative to the Cold War's bipolar world order by advocating for a policy of neutrality and non-alignment with either the United States or the Soviet Union. The principles outlined at Bandung—respect for sovereignty, non-interference, equality, and peaceful coexistence—resonated with many countries across Asia, Africa, and Latin America, which saw the movement as a platform to amplify their voices in global affairs.

For Southeast Asia, the Bandung Conference and the subsequent formation of the NAM were instrumental in fostering a sense of solidarity and unity among newly independent states. It also helped these countries navigate the complexities of Cold War geopolitics, allowing them to assert their independence and pursue development agendas without aligning with either superpower.

Political and Social Transformations Following Independence

The independence movements in Southeast Asia ushered in a period of significant political and social transformations. In Indonesia, the post-independence era was marked by a series of political upheavals, including regional rebellions, economic crises, and the establishment of an authoritarian regime under Sukarno's "Guided Democracy." The subsequent rise of Suharto's New Order regime in 1965, following a failed coup attempt, led to a shift towards military-led governance, marked by political repression and economic modernization.

In Vietnam, the struggle for independence from French colonial rule was followed by a bitter conflict between North and South Vietnam, culminating in the Vietnam War. The war, which lasted from 1955 to 1975, had a profound impact on Vietnam's social fabric, economy, and political landscape. The eventual victory of the North Vietnamese forces led to the reunification of Vietnam under communist rule, setting the stage for decades of isolation and economic hardship, followed by gradual economic reforms and international integration in the late 20th century.

Other Southeast Asian countries, such as Burma (Myanmar), Malaysia, and the Philippines, also underwent significant political changes following independence. These changes were often shaped by internal ethnic and religious dynamics, regional geopolitics, and the broader Cold War context. The legacy of colonialism, combined with the challenges of nation-building and development, created a complex political landscape in Southeast Asia, characterized by both democratic transitions and authoritarian regimes.

The independence movements in Southeast Asia were not merely a struggle for political freedom but a quest for identity, self-determination, and development in a rapidly changing world. The region's decolonization process was shaped by local dynamics, colonial legacies, and global geopolitical shifts, particularly the impact of World War II and the Cold War. The emergence of independent states in Southeast Asia, marked by the struggles in Indonesia and Vietnam, reshaped the regional political landscape and had a lasting impact on global politics.

The Bandung Conference and the formation of the Non-Aligned Movement underscored Southeast Asia's pivotal role in the broader decolonization movement, highlighting the region's desire for sovereignty, peace, and cooperation in the face of global superpower rivalries. The political and social transformations that followed independence continue to influence Southeast Asia's development trajectory, presenting both opportunities and challenges for the region in the 21st century.

Chapter 3: Decolonization in the Middle East

Introduction: The Shifting Sands of Power

Decolonization in the Middle East was a complex and multifaceted process shaped by the decline of the Ottoman Empire, the imposition of European mandates, the rise of nationalist movements, and the geopolitical ambitions of global powers. The region, long a crossroads of civilizations and a strategic fulcrum between East and West, saw its political landscape dramatically altered in the first half of the 20th century. This chapter explores the decolonization efforts in the Middle East, focusing on the struggles for independence in countries such as Egypt, Iraq, and Syria. We will examine key events like the Suez Crisis of 1956, the impact of Zionism, the creation of Israel, and the enduring conflicts that have shaped the region's postcolonial legacy. These transformations must be understood within the broader context of Cold War geopolitics, which further complicated the decolonization process in this volatile region.

The Decline of the Ottoman Empire and European Mandates

The decline of the Ottoman Empire, often referred to as "the sick man of Europe," set the stage for the decolonization struggles that would engulf the Middle East in the early 20th century. By the early 1900s, the Ottoman Empire, which had ruled much of the Middle East for centuries, was in a state of terminal decline, weakened by internal strife, economic troubles, and military defeats. World War I dealt the final blow to the Ottoman Empire, which allied itself with the Central Powers and faced defeat at the hands of the Allies. The post-war settlement dismantled the Ottoman territories in the Middle East, with the victorious Allied powers, particularly Britain and France, carving up the region into spheres of influence.

The Treaty of Sèvres in 1920 and the subsequent Treaty of Lausanne in 1923 formalized the partitioning of the Ottoman territories, leading to the establishment of European mandates under the auspices of the League of Nations. The mandate system was ostensibly designed to prepare former Ottoman territories for self-governance, but in practice, it allowed Britain and France to exert direct control over strategically important regions. Britain assumed control over Palestine, Transjordan, and Iraq, while France took over Syria and Lebanon. These mandates set the stage for nationalist movements that would challenge European rule and seek independence.

Struggles for Independence in Egypt, Iraq, and Syria

Egypt: The Birthplace of Arab Nationalism

Egypt's struggle for independence was among the earliest and most significant in the Middle East, setting a precedent for other countries in the region. Although formally a protectorate of Britain since 1882, Egypt remained a focal point of anti-colonial sentiment and nationalist fervor. The 1919 Egyptian Revolution, sparked by the British arrest of nationalist leaders like Saad Zaghloul, led to widespread protests, strikes, and civil disobedience across the country. The revolution marked a turning point in Egypt's struggle for independence, forcing Britain to negotiate with Egyptian nationalists.

In 1922, Britain unilaterally declared Egypt's independence, but retained significant control over its foreign policy, military, and the Suez Canal, a vital strategic waterway. The interwar period saw continued tensions between the Egyptian monarchy, nationalist movements, and the British, culminating in the Free Officers Movement's coup in 1952. Led by General Muhammad Naguib and later by Gamal Abdel Nasser, the coup overthrew King Farouk and established a republic, marking the end of the British-backed monarchy. Nasser emerged as a charismatic leader who sought to modernize Egypt and assert its independence from Western influence, playing a pivotal role in shaping the region's political landscape.

Iraq: From Mandate to Monarchy and Beyond

Iraq's path to independence was shaped by both internal dynamics and British strategic interests. Under the British mandate, Iraq was governed through a combination of direct rule and local client leaders, which bred resentment among nationalist groups. The discovery of oil in the region further complicated Iraq's relationship with Britain, as it became clear that control over Iraqi oil resources was a priority for the British government.

The 1920 Iraqi Revolt against British rule was a significant event that demonstrated widespread opposition to foreign domination.

Although the revolt was suppressed, it forced Britain to rethink its strategy in Iraq. In 1921, the British installed Faisal I, a Hashemite prince, as the King of Iraq, establishing a constitutional monarchy under British tutelage. Despite gaining formal independence in 1932, Iraq remained under significant British influence, especially concerning its foreign policy and military affairs.

The Second World War brought renewed tensions to Iraq, with nationalist leaders advocating for complete independence and the removal of British influence. A coup in 1941 briefly brought a pro-Axis government to power, leading to a British military intervention and occupation. After the war, Iraq continued to experience political instability, culminating in the 1958 coup led by the Free Officers Movement, which overthrew the monarchy and established a republic. This coup marked the beginning of a new era in Iraqi politics, characterized by military rule, coups, and the emergence of the Ba'ath Party.

Syria: The Fight Against French Mandate

Syria's struggle for independence from French colonial rule was marked by both armed resistance and political maneuvering. Following World War I, Syria was placed under a French mandate, much to the dismay of Syrian nationalists who had hoped for independence. The imposition of French rule sparked widespread discontent and resistance, leading to a series of uprisings, including the Great Syrian Revolt of 1925-1927, which was brutally suppressed by French forces.

The interwar period saw continued agitation for independence, with nationalist leaders like Shukri al-Quwatli and Hashim al-Atassi playing key roles in organizing resistance against French rule. The political landscape in Syria was characterized by a complex interplay of sectarian, regional, and ideological forces, which the French often manipulated to maintain control.

World War II and the subsequent collapse of the Vichy regime in France created an opening for Syrian nationalists. In 1941, Free

French forces, with British support, took control of Syria and promised eventual independence. However, it was not until 1946, after sustained pressure from Syrian nationalists and the growing international consensus on decolonization, that French troops finally withdrew, and Syria became fully independent.

The Suez Crisis of 1956: A Turning Point in Middle Eastern Decolonization

The Suez Crisis of 1956 was a watershed moment in the decolonization of the Middle East, marking the end of Britain and France's direct influence in the region and the rise of the United States and the Soviet Union as dominant powers. The crisis was precipitated by Egyptian President Gamal Abdel Nasser's decision to nationalize the Suez Canal, previously controlled by a British-French company. Nasser's move was motivated by a desire to assert Egypt's sovereignty, fund the Aswan High Dam project, and respond to the withdrawal of American and British funding for the dam.

The nationalization of the Suez Canal sparked a military response from Britain, France, and Israel, which launched a joint invasion of Egypt in October 1956. However, the invasion faced immediate condemnation from both the United States and the Soviet Union, who demanded a ceasefire. Under intense international pressure, including a financial crisis in Britain and the threat of Soviet intervention, the invading forces withdrew, and a UN peacekeeping force was deployed to oversee the withdrawal.

The Suez Crisis was a humiliation for Britain and France, signaling the end of their imperial ambitions in the Middle East. For Nasser and other nationalist leaders, the crisis was a triumph that demonstrated the possibility of successfully challenging colonial powers and asserting national sovereignty. The crisis also highlighted the growing importance of the Cold War dynamics in the region, with the United States and the Soviet Union increasingly viewing the Middle East as a critical battleground for influence.

Zionism, the Creation of Israel, and Ongoing Conflicts

The creation of Israel in 1948 and the subsequent Arab-Israeli conflict have been central to the postcolonial legacy of the Middle East. The roots of the conflict lie in the rise of Zionism in the late 19th and early 20th centuries, which sought to establish a Jewish homeland in Palestine. The Balfour Declaration of 1917, in which Britain expressed support for the establishment of a "national home for the Jewish people" in Palestine, set the stage for future tensions between Jewish and Arab communities.

The end of World War II and the Holocaust accelerated Jewish immigration to Palestine, leading to increased tensions and violence between Jews and Arabs. In 1947, the United Nations proposed a partition plan to create separate Jewish and Arab states, which was accepted by the Jewish community but rejected by the Arab states and Palestinian leaders. The declaration of the State of Israel on May 14, 1948, was immediately followed by a military intervention by neighboring Arab states, marking the beginning of the first Arab-Israeli war.

The 1948 war, also known as the Nakba ("catastrophe") by Palestinians, resulted in the establishment of Israel and the displacement of hundreds of thousands of Palestinian Arabs. The conflict created a deep and enduring rift in the region, with subsequent wars in 1956, 1967, and 1973 further entrenching divisions. The Israeli-Palestinian conflict remains a central issue in Middle Eastern politics, influencing regional dynamics and international relations.

Geopolitical Significance and the Cold War Context

The decolonization of the Middle East cannot be understood without considering the broader geopolitical context of the Cold War. The region's strategic location, vast oil reserves, and political instability made it a key arena for superpower rivalry between the United States and the Soviet Union. Both powers sought to expand their influence in the region by supporting different political factions and regimes.

The United States, for its part, sought to contain Soviet influence and secure access to Middle Eastern oil. It provided military and economic support to pro-Western regimes, such as those in Saudi Arabia, Jordan, and Iran, while also attempting to broker peace in the Arab-Israeli conflict. The Eisenhower Doctrine, announced in 1957, explicitly stated that the United States would provide military and economic assistance to Middle Eastern countries resisting communist aggression.

The Soviet Union, meanwhile, supported nationalist movements and regimes that were opposed to Western imperialism. The Soviet Union provided military and economic aid to countries like Egypt, Syria, and Iraq, which adopted socialist policies and aligned themselves with the Eastern Bloc. The Cold War rivalry between the United States and the Soviet Union played a significant role in shaping the political landscape of the Middle East, influencing everything from military alliances to economic development strategies.

Decolonization in the Middle East was a complex and often tumultuous process, marked by struggles for independence, regional conflicts, and the geopolitical maneuvering of global powers. The decline of the Ottoman Empire, the imposition of European mandates, and the rise of nationalist movements set the stage for a new era in the region's history. The Suez Crisis of 1956, the creation of Israel, and the ongoing Arab-Israeli conflict have had lasting impacts on the region's political landscape, shaping its postcolonial legacy and its role in global affairs.

As the Cold War unfolded, the Middle East became a critical arena for superpower rivalry, with both the United States and the Soviet Union vying for influence. This geopolitical context further complicated the decolonization process, influencing the region's political and social developments. The decolonization of the Middle East remains a pivotal chapter in the broader story of global decolonization, reflecting the complexities and challenges of achieving independence in a rapidly changing world.

Part 2: The Struggle for Independence in Africa

Chapter 4: West Africa's Road to Freedom

Introduction: The Dawn of Independence in West Africa

West Africa's journey to independence is a story of resilience, determination, and a deep desire for self-determination that spread across the region like wildfire in the mid-20th century. As the winds of decolonization swept across the globe, West Africa became a significant theater in the fight against colonial rule. The region, with its diverse cultures and rich histories, had long been under European domination, particularly by the British and the French. This chapter delves into West Africa's path to independence, with a focus on Ghana, the first Sub-Saharan African country to gain independence under the leadership of Kwame Nkrumah. We will explore Nkrumah's Pan-African vision, the ripple effect of Ghana's independence on neighboring countries, and the post-independence challenges these new nations faced in their quest for stability, economic development, and international recognition.

Ghana: The Trailblazer for Independence in Sub-Saharan Africa

The Rise of Kwame Nkrumah and the Fight for Freedom

The Gold Coast, known today as Ghana, was at the forefront of the independence movement in West Africa. British colonial rule had been established in the mid-19th century, and by the early 20th century, nationalist sentiments began to take root among the educated elite and broader population. The struggle for independence gained significant momentum after World War II, as the economic hardships and racial discrimination experienced by returning African soldiers fueled demands for freedom.

Kwame Nkrumah emerged as a pivotal figure in this struggle. Educated in the United States and Britain, Nkrumah was heavily influenced by the ideas of Pan-Africanism and socialism. Upon his return to the Gold Coast in 1947, he quickly became a leading voice in the independence movement. Nkrumah's dynamic leadership and charismatic oratory skills helped to galvanize mass support across the colony.

In 1949, Nkrumah formed the Convention People's Party (CPP) with a clear agenda for "self-government now." The CPP's strategy was rooted in nonviolent resistance, mass mobilization, and civil disobedience. Nkrumah's call for "Positive Action" — a series of strikes, boycotts, and protests — challenged British colonial authority and demonstrated the widespread desire for independence. The colonial government's decision to arrest Nkrumah in 1950 backfired, as it only heightened his popularity and further mobilized the masses.

The turning point came in 1951 when the British allowed limited self-governance and conducted elections for a Legislative Assembly. The CPP won a decisive victory, and although still in prison, Nkrumah was released to become the Leader of Government Business, and later, the Prime Minister. Nkrumah's leadership and his ability to negotiate with the British paved the way for Ghana's full independence, which was finally achieved on March 6, 1957.

Impact of Ghana's Independence on Pan-Africanism and Regional Movements

Ghana's independence had a profound impact on the African continent. It was not just a victory for the people of Ghana but a beacon of hope and inspiration for all colonized nations in Africa. Nkrumah, a strong advocate of Pan-Africanism, envisioned Ghana's independence as the first step towards the liberation of the entire African continent. He famously declared, "The independence of Ghana is meaningless unless it is linked up with the total liberation of the African continent."

Under Nkrumah's leadership, Ghana became a hub for Pan-African activities. Nkrumah invited and supported liberation movements from across Africa, providing financial, moral, and political support to anti-colonial activists. The All-African Peoples' Conference held in Accra in 1958 brought together representatives from various African territories, reinforcing the idea of a united African front against colonial rule.

The success of Ghana's independence movement had a domino effect on other West African countries still under colonial rule. It demonstrated that independence was achievable and emboldened nationalist movements in Nigeria, Senegal, Mali, and beyond. Nkrumah's Pan-African vision and support for other independence movements helped catalyze a wave of decolonization across the continent, creating a new sense of African identity and solidarity.

The Domino Effect: Independence Movements Across West Africa

Nigeria: The Giant of Africa's Path to Independence

Nigeria, the most populous country in Africa, embarked on its own path to independence in the wake of Ghana's success. British colonial rule in Nigeria was characterized by indirect rule, which leveraged traditional local leaders to govern on behalf of the British Crown. This system, however, deepened regional and ethnic divisions, setting the stage for future political challenges.

Nationalist sentiment in Nigeria began to grow in the early 20th century, led by intellectuals, trade unions, and emerging political parties. The Nigerian Youth Movement, founded in the 1930s, was one of the first organized efforts to demand greater political participation for Nigerians. After World War II, nationalist fervor intensified, driven by economic grievances, demands for civil rights, and the influence of decolonization movements elsewhere.

By the late 1940s, political parties such as the National Council of Nigeria and the Cameroons (NCNC) led by Nnamdi Azikiwe, the Action Group (AG) led by Obafemi Awolowo, and the Northern People's Congress (NPC) led by Ahmadu Bello had emerged, each representing different regions and ethnic groups. The British colonial administration initiated a series of constitutional reforms, leading to increased Nigerian participation in governance. However, regional and ethnic tensions complicated the decolonization process.

After years of negotiation and constitutional revisions, Nigeria gained independence on October 1, 1960. However, the new nation was immediately confronted with significant challenges, including managing regional and ethnic rivalries, establishing a stable political system, and addressing economic disparities. These tensions would eventually lead to a civil war in 1967, highlighting the complexities of postcolonial state-building in Africa.

Senegal and Mali: The Push for Sovereignty in French West Africa

Senegal and Mali, part of French West Africa, also followed the wave of independence sweeping the continent. French colonial rule in West Africa was characterized by a policy of assimilation, which sought to integrate Africans into French culture and political structures. This policy, however, faced resistance from African leaders who demanded greater autonomy and recognition of their unique cultural identities.

The independence movements in French West Africa were marked by both political negotiations and grassroots mobilization. Senegal, under the leadership of Léopold Sédar Senghor, a prominent intellectual and advocate for African cultural identity, pursued a path of political negotiation and cooperation with the French government. In 1959, Senegal and French Sudan (now Mali) formed the Mali Federation, a short-lived experiment in regional unity that dissolved in 1960 due to political disagreements.

Senegal gained full independence on April 4, 1960, with Senghor becoming the country's first president. Senghor's leadership was marked by a focus on nation-building, cultural renewal, and economic development. He promoted the philosophy of Negritude, which emphasized the value of African culture and identity, and worked to create a stable, democratic political system.

Mali, led by Modibo Keïta, took a more radical approach to independence, pursuing a socialist path and seeking to distance itself from French influence. Mali gained independence on September 22, 1960, and under Keïta's leadership, the country adopted policies of nationalization, state control of the economy, and non-alignment in the Cold War. However, Mali faced significant economic challenges and political instability, which eventually led to a military coup in 1968.

Post-Independence Challenges in West Africa

The newly independent nations of West Africa faced a myriad of challenges as they sought to consolidate their sovereignty and build stable, prosperous societies. While independence brought political freedom, it also revealed deep-seated issues stemming from colonial rule, including political instability, economic dependency, and social divisions.

Political Instability and Governance Challenges

Political instability was a common feature in many West African countries in the post-independence period. The legacy of colonial rule, which often involved dividing and ruling through ethnic and regional lines, left many new nations with weak political institutions and deep social cleavages. In countries like Nigeria, Ghana, and Mali, the lack of experience in self-governance, coupled with ethnic and regional rivalries, led to political turbulence, military coups, and, in some cases, civil wars.

Ghana, under Nkrumah, initially experienced political stability and economic growth, but Nkrumah's increasingly authoritarian rule and ambitious development projects strained the economy and led to political unrest. In 1966, Nkrumah was overthrown in a military coup, ushering in a period of political instability and frequent changes in government.

In Nigeria, regional and ethnic tensions, particularly between the North, dominated by the Hausa-Fulani, and the South, dominated by the Yoruba and Igbo, led to political conflicts and eventually the Nigerian Civil War (1967-1970). The war, also known as the Biafran War, was a tragic and bloody conflict that resulted in significant loss of life and highlighted the challenges of nation-building in a diverse society.

Economic Dependency and Development Struggles

Economic dependency on former colonial powers and the challenges of building self-sustaining economies were major obstacles for newly independent West African nations. The economies of many West African countries were heavily reliant on the export of a few primary commodities, such as cocoa, coffee, and minerals, making them vulnerable to global market fluctuations. The lack of industrialization and infrastructure, combined with the legacy of colonial economic policies that favored extractive industries, posed significant barriers to economic development.

In Ghana, Nkrumah's ambitious development plans, which included large-scale industrial projects and infrastructure development, initially showed promise but eventually led to economic difficulties. The costs of these projects, combined with falling cocoa prices, Ghana's primary export, strained the economy and contributed to growing dissatisfaction with Nkrumah's government.

Senegal and Mali, like many other West African countries, also faced economic challenges in the post-independence period. Both countries had to navigate the complexities of building independent economies while managing limited resources, a lack of infrastructure, and dependence on foreign aid and investment. In Mali, Keïta's socialist policies and attempts at economic reform met with limited success, leading to economic stagnation and political unrest.

Cold War Pressures and Geopolitical Realities

The Cold War added another layer of complexity to West Africa's post-independence struggles. The geopolitical competition between the United States and the Soviet Union meant that newly independent countries were often caught in the crossfire of Cold War politics. Both superpowers sought to expand their influence in Africa by supporting different regimes, movements, and factions.

Many West African countries adopted a policy of non-alignment, seeking to avoid becoming pawns in the Cold War. However, this was not always possible, as Cold War rivalries often played out in regional conflicts and internal political struggles. In Ghana, Nkrumah's Pan-African and socialist leanings drew the attention of both the Soviet Union, which provided support, and the United States, which viewed his policies with suspicion.

In countries like Nigeria and Senegal, leaders sought to navigate the Cold War's geopolitical landscape by maintaining a degree of neutrality and seeking economic aid and investment from both the Western and Eastern blocs. However, the pressures of Cold War politics often influenced domestic policies and exacerbated internal conflicts.

Conclusion: The Legacy of Independence in West Africa

The road to independence in West Africa was a complex and often tumultuous journey, marked by struggles for freedom, the quest for self-determination, and the challenges of building new nations. Ghana's independence in 1957 under Kwame Nkrumah was a watershed moment that inspired a wave of decolonization across the continent, setting in motion a domino effect that saw the emergence of new nations from the ashes of colonial rule.

However, the post-independence period revealed the deep-seated challenges inherited from colonialism, including political instability, economic dependency, and social divisions. The newly independent nations of West Africa had to navigate a difficult path, balancing the demands of nation-building with the realities of economic development and geopolitical pressures.

Despite these challenges, the independence movements in West Africa were a testament to the resilience and determination of its people to achieve freedom and build a better future. The legacy of these struggles continues to shape the region's political and economic landscape today, offering lessons in the complexities of postcolonial development and the enduring quest for sovereignty and self-determination.

Chapter 5: The Algerian War of Independence

Introduction: A Fight for Freedom and Identity

The Algerian War of Independence (1954-1962) was one of the most violent and protracted conflicts of the decolonization era, marking a pivotal chapter in the history of both Algeria and France. The war was not only a struggle for national independence but also a fight for identity, sovereignty, and the end of more than a century of French colonial rule. Algeria's path to independence was marked by brutal guerrilla warfare, political maneuvering, and significant social and political upheaval. This chapter explores the origins of the Algerian nationalist movement, the conflict between the National Liberation Front (FLN) and French forces, the political negotiations leading to the Evian Accords, and the long-lasting legacy of the war on both Algeria and France.

Background: French Colonial Rule and the Roots of Nationalism in Algeria

The Colonial Experience in Algeria

French colonial rule in Algeria began in 1830 with the invasion of Algiers, and over the next several decades, France expanded its control over the entire territory. Unlike many other French colonies, Algeria was not merely a protectorate or overseas territory; it was considered an integral part of France, with three departments established in 1848. The French government encouraged European settlement, and by the mid-20th century, nearly one million French settlers, known as pieds-noirs, lived in Algeria, alongside a Muslim majority population of about nine million.

The colonial regime in Algeria was characterized by systematic discrimination, economic exploitation, and political disenfranchisement of the indigenous population. French settlers controlled the best agricultural land, while the majority of Algerians lived in poverty, with limited access to education, healthcare, and political representation. French policies promoted cultural assimilation, attempting to impose French language, customs, and legal structures while undermining indigenous culture and religious practices.

The inequality and oppression inherent in the colonial system sowed the seeds of resistance and nationalism among the Algerian population. Early nationalist movements began to emerge in the 1920s and 1930s, advocating for greater rights and recognition within the French Empire. Organizations such as the Étoile Nord-Africaine (North African Star), founded by Messali Hadj, and the Association des Oulémas Musulmans Algériens (Association of Algerian Muslim Scholars), led by Sheikh Abdelhamid Ben Badis, sought to promote political, cultural, and religious rights for Algerians.

The Rise of Algerian Nationalism

The end of World War II marked a turning point in the struggle for independence in Algeria. The war had weakened European colonial powers and inspired nationalist movements worldwide. In Algeria, the war's aftermath saw a growing demand for political and social reforms. The May 1945 Sétif and Guelma massacres, in which French forces brutally suppressed peaceful demonstrations calling for independence, resulted in thousands of Algerian deaths and marked a radicalization of the nationalist movement.

The failure of peaceful reform efforts and the increasing repression by the French colonial authorities convinced many Algerians that only armed struggle could achieve independence. In 1954, a group of young nationalists, including Ahmed Ben Bella, Hocine Aït Ahmed, and Mohamed Boudiaf, formed the National Liberation Front (FLN). The FLN called for an armed uprising against French rule, marking the beginning of the Algerian War of Independence.

The War Begins: The FLN's Fight for Liberation
Guerrilla Tactics and the FLN's Strategy

The Algerian War officially began on November 1, 1954, when the FLN launched a series of coordinated attacks against French military and civilian targets throughout Algeria, an event known as the Toussaint Rouge (Red All Saints' Day). The FLN's strategy relied heavily on guerrilla tactics, leveraging Algeria's rugged terrain and the support of local populations to conduct hit-and-run attacks, ambushes, and sabotage operations against French forces.

The FLN divided Algeria into six military zones, each led by a regional commander known as a wilaya. This decentralized structure allowed the FLN to operate with flexibility and adapt to the evolving military situation. The FLN also sought to build a parallel state structure, establishing local governance, judicial systems, and tax collection in areas under its control. The aim was not only to weaken the French military presence but also to demonstrate the FLN's capacity to govern and gain the support of the Algerian population.

The FLN's use of guerrilla warfare was brutal and effective, targeting both military and civilian infrastructure. The conflict quickly escalated into a full-scale war, characterized by cycles of violence and reprisal. The FLN's campaign also included a psychological component, aiming to demoralize French forces and provoke a heavy-handed response that would alienate the local population and attract international sympathy for the Algerian cause.

French Military Response and the Brutality of War

The French government initially underestimated the strength and resolve of the FLN, viewing the conflict as a minor insurrection. However, as the conflict intensified, France deployed a massive military force to Algeria, eventually reaching over 500,000 troops. The French military strategy focused on counterinsurgency operations, which included search-and-destroy missions, intelligence gathering, and efforts to win "hearts and minds" among the Algerian population.

The French response was marked by a heavy reliance on brutal tactics, including the widespread use of torture, summary executions, and mass detentions. The French military, led by General Jacques Massu and Colonel Marcel Bigeard, conducted a brutal campaign of repression, particularly during the Battle of Algiers in 1957. The Battle of Algiers was a significant turning point in the war, as the French forces successfully dismantled the FLN's urban network in the capital through a combination of intelligence operations, curfews, and psychological warfare.

However, the methods employed by the French, particularly the use of torture and repression, had a profound impact on French society and politics. The revelations of widespread human rights abuses sparked a public outcry and led to deep divisions within French society, contributing to a growing anti-war movement. Prominent intellectuals, journalists, and political leaders began to question the morality and legitimacy of the war, leading to increased calls for a negotiated settlement.

Political Negotiations and the Path to Independence
The Road to the Evian Accords

By the late 1950s, it became clear that the war in Algeria was unwinnable for France through military means alone. The conflict was taking a heavy toll on French resources and had become a significant political and moral crisis. In 1958, amid a political crisis in France, Charles de Gaulle returned to power as President, promising to restore order and resolve the Algerian conflict.

Initially, de Gaulle appeared committed to maintaining French control over Algeria. However, recognizing the futility of a military solution and the growing international condemnation of French actions, he began to shift towards a policy of self-determination. De Gaulle's famous 1959 speech, in which he declared, "Je vous ai compris" ("I have understood you"), signaled a new direction in French policy, opening the door for negotiations with the FLN.

Negotiations between the French government and the FLN began in earnest in 1960, despite ongoing violence. The talks were complicated by hardline factions on both sides and by the presence of the pieds-noirs and other European settlers in Algeria, who vehemently opposed any concessions to the FLN. The OAS (Organisation Armée Secrète), a paramilitary group of French settlers, launched a campaign of terror against both the FLN and the French government, further complicating the negotiations.

Despite these challenges, the negotiations culminated in the signing of the Evian Accords on March 18, 1962. The Evian Accords provided for a ceasefire, the withdrawal of French troops, and the recognition of Algerian independence. The accords also included provisions for the protection of the European minority in Algeria and for economic and cultural cooperation between Algeria and France.

Independence and the Birth of a New Nation

On July 1, 1962, a national referendum was held in Algeria, with an overwhelming majority voting in favor of independence. Two days later, on July 3, 1962, France formally recognized Algerian independence, ending 132 years of colonial rule. Algeria's independence was greeted with widespread jubilation, but it also came at a high cost. The war had resulted in significant loss of life, with estimates of over a million Algerians killed and many more displaced. The conflict had also left deep scars on Algerian society, with widespread destruction and a legacy of trauma.

Algeria's independence marked a turning point in the history of decolonization in Africa and had a profound impact on both Algeria and France. The new nation faced immense challenges in its early years, including political instability, economic hardship, and the task of building a cohesive national identity. Ahmed Ben Bella, a prominent leader of the FLN, became Algeria's first President, but his tenure was marked by internal divisions and political struggles.

The War's Lasting Legacy on Algeria and France
Impact on Algeria: Challenges of Nation-Building

The legacy of the Algerian War of Independence on Algeria has been profound and enduring. The newly independent state faced significant challenges in its early years, including rebuilding a war-torn economy, integrating a diverse society, and establishing a stable political system. The war had left deep social and economic scars, with widespread poverty, unemployment, and displacement.

Politically, Algeria adopted a socialist orientation, with the FLN consolidating power and establishing a one-party state. The new government embarked on ambitious programs of land reform, nationalization of key industries, and state-led economic development. However, the legacy of colonialism, coupled with internal divisions within the FLN and the broader Algerian society, led to political instability and authoritarianism.

The war also left a deep psychological impact on Algerian society. The trauma of the conflict, coupled with the challenges of post-independence nation-building, created a complex environment characterized by both pride in the achievement of independence and frustration with the difficulties of realizing the promises of the liberation struggle.

Impact on France: A Divided Society and Political Transformation

The Algerian War of Independence had a profound impact on French society and politics, leading to deep divisions and a reevaluation of France's role as a colonial power. The war exposed the contradictions of French republican ideals of liberty, equality, and fraternity, particularly in light of the widespread use of torture, repression, and human rights abuses by French forces.

The revelations of the brutality of the war sparked widespread public outcry and led to a significant anti-war movement in France. Intellectuals, journalists, and political leaders, such as Jean-Paul Sartre and Albert Camus, openly criticized the war and called for an end to the conflict. The war also led to a political crisis in France, contributing to the collapse of the Fourth Republic and the establishment of the Fifth Republic under Charles de Gaulle.

The end of the war and the loss of Algeria forced France to confront its colonial past and its future as a nation. The return of the pieds-noirs and the Harkis (Algerians who had fought for the French) to mainland France created social tensions and challenges, as these groups faced discrimination and marginalization.

In the long term, the Algerian War of Independence has had a lasting impact on French politics and society, influencing debates on immigration, identity, and the legacy of colonialism. The war remains a sensitive and contested issue in both countries, reflecting the deep scars left by the conflict and the enduring challenges of reconciliation and memory.

The Algerian War of Independence was one of the most significant and brutal conflicts of the decolonization era, marking a turning point in the history of both Algeria and France. The war was a struggle for national liberation, identity, and sovereignty, characterized by intense violence, guerrilla warfare, and political maneuvering. The conflict had a profound impact on both countries, shaping their postcolonial trajectories and leaving a lasting legacy that continues to influence their politics and societies today.

The war's end and Algeria's independence marked the culmination of a long struggle for freedom, but it also highlighted the complexities and challenges of decolonization. The legacy of the war remains a powerful reminder of the costs of colonialism and the enduring quest for justice, sovereignty, and self-determination. As we continue to explore the broader story of decolonization across Africa and the world, the Algerian experience offers important lessons on the struggles, sacrifices, and challenges involved in the fight for independence and the building of new nations.

Chapter 6: Southern Africa's Liberation Struggles

Introduction: The Winds of Change in Southern Africa

The liberation struggles in Southern Africa were marked by a fierce determination to end colonial rule and racial oppression. Unlike other regions in Africa, where independence was often achieved through negotiations and political compromise, Southern Africa's path to freedom was paved with prolonged armed conflicts, mass mobilization, and intense international pressure. This chapter explores the complex and multifaceted liberation movements in Southern Africa, focusing on the struggles for independence in Zambia, Zimbabwe, and Mozambique, and the prolonged battle against apartheid in South Africa. We will examine the roles of key leaders such as Kenneth Kaunda, Robert Mugabe, Samora Machel, and Nelson Mandela, and discuss the impact of international solidarity, sanctions, and diplomatic efforts in these countries' quests for freedom. Finally, we will reflect on the post-independence challenges faced by these nations as they sought to build new societies free from colonial and racial oppression.

Zambia: Kenneth Kaunda and the Road to Independence

The Formation of Nationalist Movements

Zambia, known as Northern Rhodesia during the colonial period, was a British protectorate rich in copper resources. The exploitation of these resources and the accompanying racial discrimination against Africans fueled growing discontent and the rise of nationalist movements in the 1950s. The African National Congress (ANC) of Northern Rhodesia, formed in 1948, was one of the earliest political organizations advocating for African rights and independence.

Kenneth Kaunda, a charismatic teacher and activist, emerged as a leading figure in the nationalist movement. In 1958, after a split from the ANC due to disagreements over strategy, Kaunda founded the Zambia African National Congress (ZANC), which was soon banned by the colonial authorities. In response, Kaunda and his supporters formed the United National Independence Party (UNIP) in 1959, which quickly gained mass support across the territory.

The Struggle for Independence

Kaunda's leadership was marked by a commitment to nonviolent resistance, inspired by Mahatma Gandhi's philosophy of peaceful protest. Under his leadership, UNIP organized mass rallies, civil disobedience, and strikes, demanding self-government and an end to racial discrimination. The British colonial government initially resisted these demands, but the rising tide of nationalist sentiment, coupled with international pressure, led to a gradual shift in policy.

The path to independence was not without obstacles. The British sought to create a federation of Rhodesia and Nyasaland, which would include present-day Zambia, Zimbabwe, and Malawi, to maintain control over the region. However, the federation was deeply unpopular among Africans, who saw it as an attempt to entrench white minority rule. The federation's collapse in 1963 marked a turning point, paving the way for Zambia's independence.

On October 24, 1964, Zambia achieved independence, with Kenneth Kaunda becoming the country's first President. Zambia's independence was a significant victory for the nationalist movement in Southern Africa and served as a catalyst for other liberation movements in the region. Under Kaunda's leadership, Zambia became a strong supporter of liberation movements across Africa, providing sanctuary, financial support, and diplomatic backing to groups fighting against colonial rule and apartheid.

Zimbabwe: Robert Mugabe and the Fight Against White Minority Rule

Colonial Rule and the Rise of Nationalism

Zimbabwe, formerly known as Southern Rhodesia, was another British colony where the struggle for independence was long and arduous. Unlike Zambia, where independence was achieved relatively peacefully, Zimbabwe's path to freedom was characterized by a brutal guerrilla war against white minority rule. The roots of this conflict lay in the discriminatory policies of the colonial administration, which favored the small white settler population and marginalized the African majority.

The nationalist movement in Zimbabwe began to gain momentum in the 1950s, with the formation of the Southern Rhodesia African National Congress (SRANC) and, later, the Zimbabwe African People's Union (ZAPU) led by Joshua Nkomo. However, the colonial government responded to these movements with repression, banning political organizations and imprisoning their leaders. In 1963, a faction led by Robert Mugabe broke away from ZAPU to form the Zimbabwe African National Union (ZANU), which adopted a more militant stance, advocating for armed struggle against the settler regime.

The Armed Struggle and Guerrilla Warfare

The Unilateral Declaration of Independence (UDI) by the white minority government of Ian Smith in 1965 marked the beginning of a new phase in the liberation struggle. The UDI, which declared Southern Rhodesia an independent state under white minority rule, was not recognized by Britain or the international community and led to economic sanctions. However, these measures did little to change the situation on the ground, and the Smith regime remained defiant.

In response, ZANU and ZAPU launched an armed struggle against the Rhodesian government, forming military wings—the Zimbabwe African National Liberation Army (ZANLA) for ZANU and the Zimbabwe People's Revolutionary Army (ZIPRA) for ZAPU. The guerrilla war, also known as the Second Chimurenga, intensified in the 1970s, with guerrilla fighters launching attacks from bases in neighboring Mozambique and Zambia.

The liberation struggle was characterized by a combination of guerrilla warfare, diplomatic efforts, and mass mobilization. The guerrilla tactics employed by ZANLA and ZIPRA were effective in disrupting the Rhodesian economy and undermining the morale of the white minority government. The war also had a significant social impact, with thousands of Africans displaced and many more living in constant fear of reprisals by the Rhodesian security forces.

Negotiations and the Lancaster House Agreement

By the late 1970s, it became clear that a military solution was unlikely, and international pressure mounted for a negotiated settlement. The British government, led by Margaret Thatcher, brokered negotiations between the Rhodesian government and the nationalist movements in 1979, resulting in the Lancaster House Agreement. The agreement provided for a ceasefire, the return to legality of the African nationalist parties, and a transition to majority rule.

In 1980, Zimbabwe held its first free elections, and Robert Mugabe's ZANU-PF won a decisive victory. On April 18, 1980, Zimbabwe officially gained independence, ending nearly a century of colonial rule. Mugabe became the country's first Prime Minister, ushering in a new era of governance that sought to address the legacies of colonialism and promote social and economic development. However, Zimbabwe's post-independence period was marked by significant challenges, including political tensions, economic difficulties, and land reform controversies.

Mozambique: Samora Machel and the Fight for Liberation
Portuguese Colonial Rule and the Emergence of FRELIMO

Mozambique, like its neighbor Angola, was a Portuguese colony, and the struggle for independence was among the most protracted and violent in Southern Africa. Portuguese colonial rule in Mozambique was characterized by economic exploitation, racial discrimination, and brutal repression of any form of dissent. The Portuguese government's refusal to grant political rights or autonomy to the African population fueled growing resentment and nationalist sentiment.

The Frente de Libertação de Moçambique (FRELIMO), or Mozambique Liberation Front, was founded in 1962 under the leadership of Eduardo Mondlane, a Mozambican nationalist who sought to unite various factions of the independence movement. FRELIMO's strategy combined armed struggle with political mobilization, drawing support from rural communities and establishing bases in neighboring Tanzania.

The Armed Struggle and the Role of Samora Machel

After Mondlane's assassination in 1969, Samora Machel took over the leadership of FRELIMO and intensified the armed struggle against Portuguese colonial rule. Machel, a charismatic and determined leader, transformed FRELIMO into a formidable military force, adopting guerrilla tactics and launching attacks on Portuguese forces and infrastructure. FRELIMO's campaign was supported by other African liberation movements and socialist countries, which provided financial, military, and diplomatic assistance.

The struggle for independence in Mozambique was brutal and prolonged, with significant civilian casualties and widespread destruction. Portuguese forces, facing a determined and increasingly effective guerrilla campaign, resorted to harsh counterinsurgency measures, including the use of napalm, forced resettlement of rural populations, and widespread arrests and torture.

Independence and Postcolonial Challenges

The Carnation Revolution in Portugal in 1974, which overthrew the authoritarian Estado Novo regime, marked a turning point in the struggle for independence in Mozambique and other Portuguese colonies. The new Portuguese government, facing economic collapse and widespread opposition to the colonial wars, began negotiations with FRELIMO and other liberation movements. On June 25, 1975, Mozambique achieved independence, with Samora Machel becoming the country's first President.

However, Mozambique's post-independence period was marked by significant challenges. The new government adopted a socialist orientation, nationalizing key industries and implementing land reform. These policies, coupled with the devastation of the liberation war and a civil war with the anti-communist RENAMO movement, contributed to economic difficulties and political instability. The Cold War dynamics further complicated Mozambique's efforts to build a stable, prosperous society.

South Africa: The Struggle Against Apartheid
The Roots of Apartheid and Early Resistance

South Africa's liberation struggle was unique in its fight against apartheid, a system of institutionalized racial segregation and discrimination enforced by the white minority government. Apartheid was officially implemented in 1948, following the electoral victory of the National Party, which sought to entrench white supremacy and maintain political and economic control over the country's black majority.

The African National Congress (ANC), founded in 1912, emerged as the primary organization leading the fight against apartheid. Under leaders such as Albert Luthuli, Oliver Tambo, and later Nelson Mandela, the ANC adopted a strategy of nonviolent resistance, organizing strikes, protests, and civil disobedience campaigns. The 1952 Defiance Campaign and the adoption of the Freedom Charter in 1955 were key moments in the early resistance to apartheid.

The Turn to Armed Struggle: Umkhonto we Sizwe and the ANC

The Sharpeville Massacre in 1960, in which South African police killed 69 unarmed protesters, marked a turning point in the anti-apartheid struggle. The government's brutal response to peaceful protests convinced many within the ANC that nonviolent resistance alone would not be sufficient to overthrow apartheid. In 1961, the ANC, along with its ally the South African Communist Party (SACP), formed Umkhonto we Sizwe (MK), or "Spear of the Nation," the armed wing of the ANC, to carry out acts of sabotage against government infrastructure.

The ANC's turn to armed struggle marked a new phase in the liberation movement, but it also led to increased repression by the apartheid regime. Nelson Mandela and other ANC leaders were arrested and sentenced to life imprisonment in the Rivonia Trial of 1964. Despite these setbacks, the ANC continued its struggle, operating in exile and maintaining a network of underground cells within South Africa.

International Solidarity, Sanctions, and the Global Anti-Apartheid Movement

The fight against apartheid gained significant international support, with a global anti-apartheid movement emerging in the 1960s and 1970s. The movement, composed of activists, trade unions, churches, and governments, called for comprehensive economic and cultural sanctions against the apartheid regime. The United Nations imposed arms embargoes, and numerous countries and companies divested from South Africa, exerting economic pressure on the regime.

The international solidarity movement played a crucial role in sustaining the anti-apartheid struggle, providing financial support to liberation movements, raising awareness about the brutality of apartheid, and lobbying for sanctions and boycotts. The cultural boycott, which included sports, academics, and entertainment, isolated

South Africa and delegitimized the apartheid regime on the global stage.

The End of Apartheid and the Birth of a New South Africa

By the late 1980s, a combination of internal resistance, economic decline, and international pressure forced the apartheid regime to reconsider its position. In 1990, President F.W. de Klerk announced the unbanning of the ANC and other liberation movements and the release of Nelson Mandela from prison after 27 years. These steps paved the way for negotiations between the apartheid government and the liberation movements.

The negotiations, which lasted from 1990 to 1994, were fraught with challenges, including political violence, deep mistrust, and differing visions for the future of South Africa. However, the determination of leaders like Nelson Mandela and F.W. de Klerk, combined with pressure from civil society and the international community, led to a historic compromise. In 1994, South Africa held its first multiracial elections, which resulted in a decisive victory for the ANC and Nelson Mandela becoming the country's first black President.

The end of apartheid and the birth of a new democratic South Africa marked a significant achievement for the liberation struggle, but it also brought to the fore the enormous challenges of reconciliation, nation-building, and economic transformation.

The Role of International Solidarity and Sanctions

The liberation struggles in Southern Africa were significantly influenced by international solidarity and sanctions. The global anti-apartheid movement, economic sanctions, and diplomatic isolation played a critical role in pressuring colonial powers and apartheid regimes to negotiate and grant independence. The support of socialist countries, non-aligned states, and international organizations, such as the Organization of African Unity (OAU) and the United

Nations, provided crucial political, financial, and military backing to liberation movements.

Sanctions, particularly against South Africa, had a significant impact, contributing to the economic decline of the apartheid regime and increasing domestic and international pressure for reform. The global movement against apartheid, which included boycotts, divestment campaigns, and cultural isolation, helped delegitimize the regime and build a broad-based coalition of support for the liberation struggle.

Post-Independence Challenges in Southern Africa

The newly independent nations of Southern Africa faced significant challenges in the post-independence period, including political instability, economic difficulties, and social divisions. The legacy of colonialism, coupled with the devastation of prolonged liberation struggles, created complex environments for nation-building and development.

In Zambia, Kenneth Kaunda's government faced economic challenges, including falling copper prices, dependence on foreign aid, and the cost of supporting liberation movements in the region. The government's policies of nationalization and state control of the economy, while initially popular, eventually led to economic decline and political discontent, culminating in Kaunda's ouster in 1991.

In Zimbabwe, Robert Mugabe's government implemented controversial land reform policies aimed at redistributing land from white farmers to black Zimbabweans. While these policies sought to address historical injustices, they were poorly implemented and led to economic collapse, hyperinflation, and political repression.

Mozambique, under FRELIMO's leadership, faced a brutal civil war with the RENAMO movement, fueled by Cold War rivalries and regional tensions. The war, which lasted until 1992, devastated the country's economy and infrastructure, leading to widespread poverty and displacement.

In South Africa, the end of apartheid brought about significant political and social changes, but the country continues to grapple with the legacy of racial inequality, economic disparity, and social division. The challenges of reconciliation, nation-building, and economic transformation remain central to South Africa's post-apartheid trajectory.

The liberation struggles in Southern Africa were marked by courage, resilience, and a fierce determination to achieve freedom and justice. The paths to independence in Zambia, Zimbabwe, Mozambique, and the fight against apartheid in South Africa were shaped by complex political, social, and economic dynamics, as well as the broader context of Cold War geopolitics and international solidarity. The liberation movements in Southern Africa succeeded in dismantling colonial and racial regimes, but the post-independence period brought new challenges of governance, economic development, and social cohesion.

The legacy of these liberation struggles continues to influence the political and social landscape of Southern Africa today, offering important lessons on the complexities of decolonization, the importance of international solidarity, and the ongoing quest for justice, equality, and self-determination. As we continue to explore the broader story of decolonization across Africa and the world, the experiences of Southern Africa provide a powerful reminder of the enduring challenges and triumphs of the fight for freedom.

Part 3: The Caribbean Quest for Independence

Chapter 7: The West Indies Federation and Caribbean Nationalism

Introduction: The Birth of Caribbean Nationalism

Caribbean nationalism and the quest for independence were central to the region's mid-20th-century political and social transformations. In the aftermath of World War II, the Caribbean, like much of the colonized world, saw a surge in nationalist sentiments as people sought to break free from colonial rule and assert their sovereignty. The West Indies Federation, formed in 1958, was a bold experiment in regional unity and cooperation among British Caribbean colonies, aiming to foster a collective path to independence and regional integration. This chapter examines the formation, goals, and challenges of the West Indies Federation, the reasons for its dissolution in 1962, and the subsequent paths to independence for Jamaica, Trinidad and Tobago, and Barbados. We will also explore the broader implications of Caribbean nationalism and the quest for identity in postcolonial societies.

The Formation of the West Indies Federation: A Dream of Unity

Background and Objectives of the Federation

The idea of a united West Indies dates back to the 19th century, but it gained significant traction in the post-World War II era as decolonization became a global phenomenon. The British government, facing increased demands for independence across its colonies, saw the potential for a federated West Indies as a means to streamline the process of decolonization, maintain influence in the region, and create a politically and economically viable entity.

The West Indies Federation was officially established on January 3, 1958, comprising ten British Caribbean colonies: Antigua and Barbuda, Barbados, Dominica, Grenada, Jamaica, Montserrat, Saint Kitts and Nevis, Saint Lucia, Saint Vincent and the Grenadines, and Trinidad and Tobago. The Federation's capital was located in Port of Spain, Trinidad, and it was governed by a federal parliament and executive council.

The primary objectives of the Federation were to promote political unity, foster economic development, and provide a collective approach to achieving independence from Britain. The leaders of the Federation believed that by pooling their resources and strengths, the Caribbean territories could form a viable political entity that would be better equipped to handle the challenges of self-governance and international relations. The Federation aimed to address common issues such as trade, defense, immigration, and social services, while also preserving the unique cultural identities of its member states.

The Challenges of Unity: Divergent Interests and Economic Realities

Despite its lofty goals, the West Indies Federation faced numerous challenges from the outset. The member territories were geographically dispersed, with significant cultural, linguistic, and economic differences. These differences were often exacerbated by historical rivalries, political disagreements, and varying levels of economic development. The larger islands, such as Jamaica and Trinidad and Tobago, had more developed economies and a greater degree of political influence, while the smaller islands were economically dependent and politically weaker.

Economic disparities among the member states posed a significant challenge to the Federation's viability. Jamaica and Trinidad and Tobago, the two largest and most economically developed territories, contributed the most to the federal budget and expected to exert greater influence over federal policies. However, this created tensions with the smaller territories, which feared domination by the larger islands. Additionally, the smaller territories were heavily reliant on British financial assistance and had limited resources to contribute to the Federation's development plans.

Political disagreements also plagued the Federation. There was no clear consensus on the ultimate goal of the Federation—whether it was to achieve full political independence from Britain as a united entity or to serve as a stepping stone towards individual independence for each member state. The lack of a unified vision, coupled with divergent political ideologies among the leaders of the member territories, created a climate of uncertainty and division.

Dissolution of the Federation: The Collapse of a Dream
Jamaica's Withdrawal and the Unraveling of the Federation

The fragile unity of the West Indies Federation began to unravel in 1961 when Jamaica, the largest and most populous member, decided to withdraw. The decision was influenced by several factors, including economic considerations, political disagreements, and a growing sense of Jamaican nationalism.

Jamaica, led by Prime Minister Norman Manley of the People's National Party (PNP), conducted a national referendum on September 19, 1961, to determine whether the island should remain in the Federation. The results were decisive: 54% of voters chose to leave the

Federation. Many Jamaicans felt that the Federation was not serving their interests and that Jamaica could achieve greater economic and political autonomy by pursuing independence on its own. The withdrawal of Jamaica was a significant blow to the Federation, as it lost its largest member and a substantial portion of its economic base.

Following Jamaica's withdrawal, the future of the Federation was thrown into doubt. The departure of Jamaica set off a chain reaction, with other member states beginning to question the viability of the Federation without its largest constituent. Trinidad and Tobago, under the leadership of Prime Minister Eric Williams, was particularly concerned about the economic burden it would have to bear as the second-largest territory. Williams famously declared, "One from ten leaves nought," emphasizing that the Federation could not survive without Jamaica.

Trinidad and Tobago's Exit and the Formal Dissolution

Trinidad and Tobago's decision to withdraw from the Federation in January 1962 was the final nail in the coffin. Williams, initially a strong supporter of the Federation, had grown increasingly skeptical of its sustainability in light of Jamaica's exit and the ongoing political and economic challenges. Faced with mounting domestic pressure to pursue an independent path, Williams announced Trinidad and Tobago's intention to leave the Federation.

The withdrawal of Jamaica and Trinidad and Tobago effectively left the remaining smaller islands with little choice but to dissolve the Federation. On May 31, 1962, the West Indies Federation was formally dissolved, ending a brief and tumultuous experiment in regional unity. The dissolution was seen as a setback for the dream of a united Caribbean, but it also paved the way for the individual independence of the member territories.

Paths to Independence: Jamaica, Trinidad and Tobago, and Barbados

Jamaica: A New Dawn of Independence

After withdrawing from the Federation, Jamaica moved quickly towards independence. The Jamaican government, led by Norman Manley, negotiated with the British government to achieve a peaceful transition to self-rule. On August 6, 1962, Jamaica became the first of the British Caribbean colonies to gain full independence, with Alexander Bustamante of the Jamaica Labour Party (JLP) serving as the country's first Prime Minister.

Jamaica's independence marked a new chapter in its history, characterized by a focus on nation-building, economic development, and the establishment of a democratic political system. However, the post-independence period also brought significant challenges, including economic disparities, political violence, and social inequalities. Jamaica's experience reflected the broader difficulties faced by newly independent Caribbean states as they sought to navigate the complexities of postcolonial governance and development.

Trinidad and Tobago: A Prosperous Island Nation

Following its withdrawal from the Federation, Trinidad and Tobago also pursued an independent path. The government of Eric Williams, a leading intellectual and advocate for Caribbean nationalism, negotiated with Britain for independence. On August 31, 1962, Trinidad and Tobago became an independent nation, with Williams as its first Prime Minister.

Trinidad and Tobago's independence was marked by optimism and a commitment to building a prosperous, democratic society. The country's relatively strong economy, buoyed by oil and natural gas resources, provided a solid foundation for development. Williams emphasized education, economic diversification, and social reform as key pillars of nation-building. However, like Jamaica, Trinidad and Tobago faced challenges in managing ethnic tensions, political divisions, and the legacies of colonialism.

Barbados: A Model of Stability and Progress

Barbados, one of the smaller members of the West Indies Federation, took a more cautious approach to independence. Under the leadership of Errol Barrow, the government pursued a gradual path toward self-rule, emphasizing economic stability, social development, and political reform. On November 30, 1966, Barbados achieved full independence from Britain, with Barrow becoming the country's first Prime Minister.

Barbados's post-independence period has been characterized by political stability, economic growth, and social progress. The country has maintained a strong democratic tradition, with regular elections and peaceful transitions of power. Barbados's emphasis on education, healthcare, and infrastructure development has contributed to its reputation as one of the most stable and prosperous countries in the Caribbean.

The Broader Implications of Caribbean Nationalism and Postcolonial Identity

The Quest for Identity and Unity in a Postcolonial Context

The dissolution of the West Indies Federation and the subsequent paths to independence for its member states underscored the complexities of Caribbean nationalism and the quest for identity in a postcolonial context. The experience of the Federation highlighted the challenges of achieving regional unity in the face of diverse cultural, economic, and political realities.

Caribbean nationalism was shaped by a unique blend of historical experiences, cultural influences, and social dynamics. The region's colonial past, characterized by slavery, indentureship, and European domination, created a complex social fabric marked by racial and ethnic diversity, cultural hybridity, and economic dependency. The quest for independence was not just a political struggle but also a cultural and psychological journey towards reclaiming a sense of identity, pride, and self-determination.

The failure of the Federation revealed the difficulties of forging a unified Caribbean identity in the face of local loyalties, economic disparities, and political divisions. However, it also demonstrated the resilience and adaptability of Caribbean societies, which sought to balance the aspirations for regional unity with the realities of national sovereignty and self-interest.

Caribbean Integration and the Legacy of the Federation

Despite its failure, the West Indies Federation left a lasting legacy in the Caribbean, shaping subsequent efforts at regional integration and cooperation. The experience of the Federation underscored the importance of collaboration and solidarity among Caribbean states in addressing common challenges and promoting sustainable development.

In the years following the Federation's dissolution, Caribbean leaders sought new avenues for regional cooperation. The Caribbean Free Trade Association (CARIFTA), established in 1965, and its successor, the Caribbean Community (CARICOM), formed in 1973, were direct responses to the need for economic integration and political collaboration. CARICOM, in particular, has played a critical role in promoting regional trade, coordinating economic policies, and addressing shared concerns such as climate change, disaster management, and security.

The spirit of Caribbean nationalism and the quest for unity remain central to the region's postcolonial identity. While the dream of a politically united West Indies may have faded, the continued efforts toward regional integration reflect a commitment to collective action, mutual support, and the shared pursuit of a better future for all Caribbean peoples.

The story of the West Indies Federation and Caribbean nationalism is a tale of both ambition and limitation, unity and division. The Federation represented a bold experiment in regional cooperation, driven by a desire to achieve independence and self-determination as a united entity. However, the challenges of divergent interests, economic disparities, and political divisions ultimately led to its dissolution.

The paths to independence for Jamaica, Trinidad and Tobago, and Barbados, along with other Caribbean nations, marked the beginning of a new era of sovereignty, nation-building, and development. The experiences of these countries reflect the broader complexities of decolonization and the quest for identity in postcolonial societies.

The legacy of Caribbean nationalism and the spirit of regional unity continue to shape the region's future. As the Caribbean navigates the challenges and opportunities of the 21st century, the lessons of the Federation and the ongoing efforts towards integration remind us of the enduring quest for unity, justice, and self-determination in a diverse and dynamic region.

Chapter 8: The Influence of Fidel Castro and the Cuban Revolution

Introduction: A Revolutionary Tide in the Caribbean

The Cuban Revolution of 1959, led by Fidel Castro, Che Guevara, and their revolutionary comrades, marked a seismic shift not only in Cuban history but also in the geopolitical landscape of the Caribbean and Latin America. The revolution's impact extended far beyond Cuba's borders, influencing political ideologies, inspiring socialist movements, and challenging the dominance of U.S. influence in the region during the Cold War. This chapter explores the rise of Fidel Castro, the overthrow of Fulgencio Batista, and the profound effects of the Cuban Revolution on neighboring countries. We will analyze the revolution's role in the Cold War dynamics, its influence on socialist movements in the region, and the long-term effects on Cuban society and its post-colonial identity.

The Rise of Fidel Castro and the Overthrow of Batista

Background: Cuba Under Batista's Rule

Cuba, under the rule of Fulgencio Batista, was characterized by economic inequality, social injustice, and political repression. Batista, who first came to power through a coup in 1933 and ruled as a strongman until 1944, returned to power in a 1952 coup after a brief period of democratic governance. His regime was marked by corruption, cronyism, and brutal suppression of political dissent. While Cuba's economy grew, largely driven by sugar exports and tourism, the benefits of this growth were unevenly distributed. Much of the wealth was concentrated among the elite and foreign investors, while a significant portion of the population lived in poverty.

Political opposition to Batista's rule grew throughout the 1950s, with increasing dissatisfaction among students, intellectuals, workers, and rural communities. Batista's ties to organized crime and his willingness to use brutal tactics to maintain power only deepened public discontent. This environment created fertile ground for a revolutionary movement that sought to overthrow the dictatorship and establish a new political order.

The Emergence of Fidel Castro and the Revolutionary Movement

Fidel Castro, a young lawyer and activist, emerged as a central figure in the opposition to Batista's regime. Born in 1926 to a wealthy landowning family, Castro became politically radicalized during his student years at the University of Havana, where he was exposed to Marxist ideas and anti-imperialist sentiments. After an unsuccessful attempt to challenge Batista through legal means, Castro turned to armed struggle as the only viable path to change.

On July 26, 1953, Castro led a group of rebels in an attack on the Moncada Barracks in Santiago de Cuba, hoping to spark a broader uprising against Batista. The attack failed, and many of the rebels were killed or captured. Castro and his brother, Raúl, were arrested and later sentenced to prison. However, the Moncada attack became a rallying cry for the Cuban opposition, and Castro's subsequent trial and imprisonment turned him into a national figure. His famous speech, "History Will Absolve Me," delivered during his trial, outlined his vision for a new Cuba free from tyranny and social inequality.

After being released from prison in 1955 as part of a general amnesty, Castro went into exile in Mexico, where he regrouped with a small band of revolutionaries, including the Argentine doctor Ernesto "Che" Guevara. Together, they formed the 26th of July Movement, named after the failed Moncada assault, and began planning an armed insurrection against Batista. In December 1956, Castro and his guerrilla fighters landed in Cuba's eastern Sierra Maestra mountains, launching a guerrilla campaign against Batista's forces.

The Triumph of the Cuban Revolution

Over the next two years, Castro's forces, composed mainly of rural peasants, workers, and disillusioned former soldiers, waged a determined guerrilla campaign against the Batista regime. The revolutionaries utilized guerrilla warfare tactics, leveraging the rugged terrain of the Sierra Maestra and winning the support of local populations through promises of land reform and social justice. The 26th of July Movement's commitment to social and economic reforms, combined with Batista's increasing brutality and repression, helped to broaden its support base among the Cuban population.

As the revolutionary movement gained momentum, urban guerrilla groups in cities like Havana and Santiago de Cuba also carried out acts of sabotage and resistance against Batista's forces. The regime's efforts to quell the rebellion through forceful measures only increased opposition, both domestically and internationally. By late 1958, Batista's hold on power had weakened significantly, and his forces were demoralized and increasingly ineffective.

On January 1, 1959, Batista fled Cuba for the Dominican Republic, and Castro's forces entered Havana triumphantly. The Cuban Revolution had succeeded, and Fidel Castro emerged as the undisputed leader of a new Cuba. The revolution's victory was celebrated by many Cubans who saw it as the dawn of a new era of freedom, equality, and social justice.

The Impact of the Cuban Revolution on the Caribbean and Latin America

The Spread of Revolutionary Ideals

The success of the Cuban Revolution sent shockwaves throughout the Caribbean and Latin America, inspiring a wave of revolutionary movements and socialist ideologies across the region. For many in Latin America, Castro's victory symbolized the possibility of overthrowing corrupt and oppressive regimes and replacing them with governments dedicated to social and economic justice. The revolution's emphasis on land reform, nationalization of foreign-owned assets, and wealth redistribution resonated with marginalized populations suffering under exploitative economic systems and dictatorial regimes.

Che Guevara, in particular, became an iconic figure of revolutionary struggle, advocating for armed insurrection as a means to achieve social change. Guevara's writings and speeches, including his famous call to create "two, three, many Vietnams," encouraged revolutionary movements to rise up against imperialism and oppression. Inspired by the Cuban example, leftist guerrilla movements emerged in countries such as Nicaragua, Colombia, Guatemala, and Bolivia, seeking to replicate Castro's success.

The Cuban Revolution and the Cold War Dynamics

The Cuban Revolution also had profound implications for the Cold War dynamics in the Western Hemisphere. The revolution's socialist orientation and the subsequent alliance with the Soviet Union challenged U.S. dominance in the region and heightened Cold War tensions. The United States, which had initially been ambivalent about Castro, quickly turned against him as his government moved to nationalize American-owned businesses and align with the Soviet bloc.

The failed Bay of Pigs invasion in 1961, an attempt by the U.S. government to overthrow Castro using Cuban exiles, further solidified Castro's resolve to resist U.S. influence. The invasion's failure embarrassed the Kennedy administration and significantly boosted Castro's standing domestically and internationally. It also deepened Castro's ties with the Soviet Union, leading to increased military and economic support from Moscow.

The Cuban Missile Crisis in October 1962 marked the peak of Cold War tensions in the region. The discovery of Soviet nuclear missiles in Cuba brought the United States and the Soviet Union to the brink of nuclear war. The crisis was ultimately resolved through a negotiated agreement in which the Soviet Union agreed to remove the missiles in exchange for a U.S. commitment not to invade Cuba and the removal of U.S. missiles from Turkey. The crisis demonstrated the extent to which Cuba had become a central player in the Cold War, capable of influencing global geopolitics.

Influence on Socialist Movements in Latin America

The Cuban Revolution had a lasting impact on socialist movements throughout Latin America. In many countries, leftist guerrilla movements adopted the Cuban model of armed struggle and sought to replicate its success. The Cuban government actively supported these movements, providing training, weapons, and financial assistance to groups fighting against right-wing dictatorships and U.S.-backed regimes.

In Nicaragua, the Sandinista National Liberation Front (FSLN) drew inspiration from the Cuban Revolution in its struggle against the Somoza dictatorship. With Cuban support, the Sandinistas eventually overthrew the Somoza regime in 1979, establishing a revolutionary government committed to social and economic reforms. Similar movements emerged in El Salvador, Guatemala, and other countries, where leftist guerrillas engaged in protracted conflicts with government forces.

However, the Cuban model also faced significant challenges and limitations. In many cases, the revolutionary movements failed to gain broad popular support, and their reliance on armed struggle alienated segments of the population. Furthermore, the U.S. government, fearing the spread of communism in its "backyard," provided substantial military and economic support to counterinsurgency efforts, leading to prolonged civil wars and significant human suffering.

Long-Term Effects of the Cuban Revolution on Cuban Society
Economic Reforms and Social Transformation

The Cuban Revolution brought about profound social and economic changes within Cuba. One of the first actions taken by Castro's government was to implement sweeping land reforms, redistributing land from large estates to landless peasants and rural workers. The government also nationalized key industries, banks, and foreign-owned assets, asserting state control over the economy. These measures were aimed at reducing inequality, promoting economic self-sufficiency, and breaking the hold of foreign economic interests over Cuba.

Social reforms were also a central focus of the revolution. The government launched ambitious programs to expand education, healthcare, and social services, with the goal of achieving universal access and improving the quality of life for all Cubans. Literacy campaigns, public health initiatives, and social welfare programs significantly improved indicators of social development, making Cuba a regional leader in education and healthcare outcomes.

However, the revolution's economic policies also faced significant challenges. The nationalization of industries and the focus on state-led development led to inefficiencies, bureaucratic mismanagement, and a lack of innovation. The U.S. embargo, imposed in 1960 and intensified in subsequent years, further exacerbated economic difficulties, isolating Cuba from key markets and sources of investment. Cuba's reliance on Soviet aid and subsidies during the Cold War created a dependency that became a major vulnerability following the collapse of the Soviet Union in 1991.

Political Repression and Human Rights Concerns

While the Cuban Revolution achieved significant social gains, it also established an authoritarian political system characterized by the centralization of power and suppression of dissent. Castro's government quickly moved to consolidate power, eliminating political opposition and curtailing civil liberties. Political parties other than the Communist Party of Cuba were banned, and the press was placed under state control.

The government's tight control over political and social life extended to various aspects of Cuban society, including religious institutions, cultural organizations, and labor unions. Critics of the regime, both domestic and international, were subjected to surveillance, harassment, imprisonment, and, in some cases, forced exile. Human rights organizations have documented numerous instances of arbitrary detention, lack of due process, and restrictions on freedom of expression and assembly in Cuba.

The Cuban government's approach to political dissent and opposition has remained a contentious issue, drawing criticism from human rights advocates and Western governments while being defended by supporters of the revolution who argue that these measures were necessary to defend the gains of the revolution and resist foreign intervention.

Cultural Revolution and National Identity

The Cuban Revolution also sought to forge a new cultural identity that was distinct from the colonial and capitalist influences of the past. The government promoted a cultural revolution that emphasized Cuban nationalism, anti-imperialism, and socialist ideals. The arts were mobilized as tools of revolutionary propaganda, and cultural institutions were tasked with promoting a new socialist consciousness.

Cuba became a hub of revolutionary culture and intellectual exchange, attracting artists, writers, and activists from across Latin America and the Global South. The government established institutions like Casa de las Américas and the Cuban Institute of Cinematographic Art and Industry (ICAIC) to promote cultural production that aligned with revolutionary values.

The promotion of Afro-Cuban culture and heritage also became a significant aspect of the Cultural Revolution. The government recognized the historical contributions of Afro-Cubans and sought to integrate Afro-Cuban traditions into the national identity. However, this cultural inclusivity was often complicated by racial and class dynamics that persisted despite official rhetoric of racial equality.

The Post-Colonial Identity of Cuba: A Complex Legacy

The Cuban Revolution's influence on the Caribbean and Latin America, and its impact on Cuban society, is marked by both achievements and contradictions. On the one hand, the revolution successfully challenged U.S. hegemony in the region, inspired generations of socialists and anti-imperialists, and achieved notable gains in education, healthcare, and social equality. On the other hand, it also established an authoritarian political system, curtailed civil liberties, and faced significant economic challenges.

The legacy of the Cuban Revolution remains a topic of intense debate and analysis. For some, Cuba represents a beacon of resistance against imperialism and a model of social development that prioritizes human welfare over profit. For others, it is a cautionary tale of authoritarianism and economic mismanagement that highlights the limitations of centralized state control and the suppression of political freedoms.

As Cuba continues to navigate the complexities of a post-Cold War world, the legacy of the revolution remains a defining element of its national identity and its place in the broader global context. The Cuban experience provides valuable insights into the challenges and possibilities of building a post-colonial society that seeks to balance social justice, political freedom, and economic sustainability.

The Cuban Revolution, led by Fidel Castro and his revolutionary comrades, was a transformative event that reshaped the political landscape of the Caribbean and Latin America. It inspired revolutionary movements, challenged U.S. dominance, and contributed to the global Cold War dynamics. The revolution's impact on Cuban society was profound, bringing significant social changes while also establishing a one-party state with a complex legacy.

The influence of the Cuban Revolution on the region and the world continues to be felt today, reflecting the enduring challenges of decolonization, the pursuit of social justice, and the quest for a post-colonial identity. As we continue to explore the broader story of decolonization and independence movements, the Cuban experience offers critical lessons on the complexities of revolutionary change and the multifaceted legacies of postcolonial transformation.

Part 4: Impact on Global Politics and Legacies of Decolonization

Chapter 9: The Non-Aligned Movement and Global South Solidarity

Introduction: A New Voice in Global Politics

The Non-Aligned Movement (NAM) emerged in the mid-20th century as a powerful coalition of newly independent states seeking to assert their sovereignty and promote peace in an increasingly polarized world. As the Cold War intensified, dividing the globe into two hostile camps led by the United States and the Soviet Union, a group of countries from Asia, Africa, and Latin America charted a different course. They sought to avoid alignment with either bloc, emphasizing independence, self-determination, and cooperation among nations of the Global South. This chapter explores the origins and objectives of the Non-Aligned Movement, key conferences that shaped its development, the role of influential leaders like Jawaharlal Nehru, Gamal Abdel Nasser, and Josip Broz Tito, and its impact on Cold War dynamics and global politics. We will also examine the movement's legacy in modern international relations and its relevance in today's multipolar world.

Origins and Objectives of the Non-Aligned Movement
The Birth of Non-Alignment: A Response to Cold War Polarization

The origins of the Non-Aligned Movement can be traced back to the early years of the Cold War, as newly independent countries in Asia, Africa, and Latin America sought to navigate a complex international landscape dominated by superpower rivalry. Many of these countries had just emerged from colonial rule and were keen to safeguard their newfound sovereignty and avoid entanglement in the geopolitical struggles of the Cold War. They were united by a shared desire to promote peace, resist neocolonialism, and pursue economic development independently of the ideological conflicts between East and West.

The concept of non-alignment was articulated by leaders such as Jawaharlal Nehru of India, Gamal Abdel Nasser of Egypt, and Josip Broz Tito of Yugoslavia, who saw it as a way to avoid being drawn into the superpower rivalry while fostering solidarity and cooperation among newly independent states. For these leaders, non-alignment was not merely a passive stance but an active commitment to peace, sovereignty, and development. It was also seen as a means to assert their countries' independence in international affairs and challenge the dominance of the superpowers.

Foundational Principles and Goals of the Movement

The Non-Aligned Movement was founded on several key principles, which were articulated in various declarations and conferences over the years. These principles included:

- **Respect for Sovereignty and Territorial Integrity:** The NAM countries emphasized the importance of maintaining sovereignty and territorial integrity, opposing any form of foreign intervention or aggression.
- **Non-Interference in Domestic Affairs:** Member states

committed to a policy of non-interference in each other's internal affairs, promoting peaceful coexistence and mutual respect.

- **Promotion of Peaceful Coexistence:** The movement sought to promote peaceful coexistence among nations, advocating for diplomacy and dialogue as the primary means of resolving conflicts.
- **Opposition to Colonialism and Neocolonialism:** The NAM was firmly anti-colonial and opposed all forms of neocolonialism, racism, and imperialism, supporting struggles for independence and self-determination worldwide.
- **Economic Development and Cooperation:** The movement aimed to foster economic cooperation and development among its members, advocating for a new international economic order that would address the inequities of the global system.

The NAM sought to provide a platform for countries of the Global South to articulate their interests, assert their sovereignty, and demand a more equitable and just international order. It was conceived as a forum for solidarity and cooperation, where newly independent states could support each other in their quest for development and self-determination.

Key Conferences and the Formation of the Non-Aligned Movement

The Bandung Conference of 1955: A Watershed Moment

The Bandung Conference, held in Indonesia in April 1955, is often considered the precursor to the Non-Aligned Movement and a defining moment in the history of postcolonial international relations. The conference brought together representatives from 29 Asian and African countries, many of which had recently gained independence or were in the process of decolonization. The leaders at Bandung, including Nehru, Nasser, Sukarno of Indonesia, and Zhou Enlai of China, sought to promote solidarity among newly independent states and assert their collective interests in global affairs.

The Bandung Conference laid the groundwork for the Non-Aligned Movement by articulating a set of principles that would later become central to the NAM's platform. The conference called for mutual respect for sovereignty, non-aggression, non-interference, equality, and peaceful coexistence. The leaders at Bandung emphasized the importance of remaining independent from the superpower blocs and resisting any form of colonial or imperial domination.

Bandung was also significant in fostering a sense of solidarity and unity among the countries of Asia and Africa, creating a shared identity based on their common experiences of colonialism and their aspirations for development and self-determination. The conference marked the beginning of a new era of cooperation among the newly independent states and set the stage for the formal establishment of the Non-Aligned Movement a few years later.

The Belgrade Conference of 1961: Formalizing the Non-Aligned Movement

The formal establishment of the Non-Aligned Movement took place at the Belgrade Conference in September 1961, hosted by Josip Broz Tito in Yugoslavia. The conference brought together 25 countries from Asia, Africa, and Latin America, including India, Egypt, Ghana, Indonesia, and Cuba. The Belgrade Conference was a culmination of years of efforts by leaders like Nehru, Nasser, and Tito to build a coalition of independent states committed to non-alignment and peaceful coexistence.

At Belgrade, the leaders of the NAM reaffirmed the principles articulated at Bandung and formally adopted them as the foundation of the movement. They declared their commitment to maintaining independence from the superpowers, promoting disarmament, and supporting the struggles for independence in Asia, Africa, and Latin America. The conference also underscored the importance of economic cooperation and development, advocating for a new international economic order that would address the inequities of the global economic system.

The Belgrade Conference marked the emergence of the Non-Aligned Movement as a significant force in international politics, providing a platform for newly independent states to assert their sovereignty, advocate for their interests, and challenge the dominance of the superpowers. The movement's commitment to non-alignment, peaceful coexistence, and economic cooperation would shape its agenda and activities in the years to come.

Influence of the Non-Aligned Movement on Cold War Dynamics

A Third Force in a Bipolar World

The Non-Aligned Movement emerged as a third force in a world divided by the Cold War, providing an alternative to the binary choice between alignment with the United States or the Soviet Union. By advocating for non-alignment, the NAM sought to break the stranglehold of superpower rivalry and create space for newly independent states to pursue their own paths to development and self-determination. The movement challenged the notion that the world had to be divided into two hostile blocs and instead promoted a vision of international relations based on cooperation, solidarity, and mutual respect.

The NAM's emphasis on non-alignment was not merely a passive stance but an active commitment to peace and independence. The movement sought to promote dialogue and diplomacy as the primary means of resolving conflicts and preventing the escalation of Cold War tensions. By refusing to align with either bloc, NAM countries positioned themselves as mediators and peace brokers, advocating for peaceful coexistence and disarmament.

Impact on Superpower Strategies and Cold War Policies

The emergence of the Non-Aligned Movement had significant implications for Cold War dynamics, influencing the strategies and policies of both the United States and the Soviet Union. The superpowers recognized that the NAM represented a substantial bloc of countries that could not be easily swayed or controlled. Both the United States and the Soviet Union sought to engage with NAM countries, offering economic aid, military assistance, and diplomatic support in an effort to gain influence and support for their respective positions.

The NAM's insistence on non-alignment and independence often put it at odds with both superpowers, particularly when it came to issues of military alliances, foreign bases, and nuclear disarmament. The movement's call for a more equitable international economic order and its support for anti-colonial and liberation movements also challenged the geopolitical and economic interests of the superpowers, particularly the United States, which viewed the spread of socialism and anti-imperialism with suspicion and hostility.

The NAM's influence was particularly evident in forums such as the United Nations, where NAM countries often coordinated their positions and voted as a bloc on issues related to decolonization, disarmament, and economic development. The movement's ability to articulate a collective voice on behalf of the Global South significantly shaped the agenda and outcomes of international organizations, forcing the superpowers to take the interests and concerns of the newly independent states into account.

The Non-Aligned Movement as a Platform for Sovereignty and Development

Advocating for Economic Justice and a New International Economic Order

One of the central concerns of the Non-Aligned Movement was economic development and the pursuit of a more just and equitable international economic order. Many NAM countries faced significant challenges in the postcolonial era, including poverty, underdevelopment, and dependence on foreign aid and investment. The movement recognized that political independence was not sufficient without economic independence and sought to address the structural inequalities in the global economic system that perpetuated neocolonialism and dependency.

The NAM advocated for a New International Economic Order (NIEO) that would address these inequalities by promoting fair trade, equitable access to markets, technology transfer, and financial assistance to developing countries. The movement called for the restructuring of international financial institutions, such as the International Monetary Fund (IMF) and the World Bank, to better represent the interests of developing countries and promote development-oriented policies.

The NAM's focus on economic justice resonated with many countries in the Global South, which saw the movement as a platform to demand greater equity and fairness in international economic relations. The movement's advocacy for a NIEO also highlighted the interconnectedness of economic development, political sovereignty, and social justice, emphasizing the need for a holistic approach to development that went beyond mere economic growth.

Providing a Voice for the Global South in International Affairs

The Non-Aligned Movement played a critical role in providing a collective voice for the Global South in international affairs. In a world dominated by the superpowers and their allies, the NAM offered an alternative platform where newly independent states could articulate their interests, share their experiences, and build solidarity. The movement provided a forum for dialogue, cooperation, and mutual support, allowing member states to coordinate their positions and present a united front on key issues.

The NAM's emphasis on sovereignty, self-determination, and non-interference resonated with many countries that had recently emerged from colonial rule and were determined to assert their independence and protect their sovereignty. The movement's commitment to peaceful coexistence and diplomacy also appealed to countries that sought to avoid becoming pawns in the superpower rivalry and instead focused on development and nation-building.

The NAM's influence extended beyond its formal membership, as its principles and objectives were embraced by other countries and movements seeking to assert their independence and promote peace and justice. The movement's impact on international affairs was particularly evident in its support for anti-colonial struggles, disarmament efforts, and the promotion of human rights and social justice.

Legacy of the Non-Aligned Movement in Modern International Relations

Relevance in a Multipolar World

The end of the Cold War and the emergence of a multipolar world order have significantly altered the global geopolitical landscape, raising questions about the relevance and role of the Non-Aligned Movement in contemporary international relations. While the bipolar rivalry that gave rise to the NAM has ended, many of the issues that the movement sought to address—such as inequality, neocolonialism, and the need for a more just international order—remain highly relevant.

In today's world, the NAM continues to provide a platform for dialogue and cooperation among developing countries, advocating for a more inclusive and equitable international system. The movement remains committed to its founding principles of non-alignment, sovereignty, and peaceful coexistence, and its agenda continues to reflect the concerns and aspirations of the Global South.

The NAM's emphasis on multilateralism, diplomacy, and dialogue also resonates in a world increasingly characterized by complex interdependence and global challenges, such as climate change, pandemics, and economic inequality. The movement's call for a more just and equitable international order and its support for the principles of international law and human rights continue to provide a valuable perspective in contemporary international relations.

Continuing Challenges and Opportunities for Solidarity

The Non-Aligned Movement faces several challenges in the 21st century, including the need to adapt to new geopolitical realities, address internal divisions, and enhance its effectiveness as a platform for advocacy and action. The movement must also grapple with issues of relevance and representation, as it seeks to represent a diverse and evolving Global South in an increasingly complex and interconnected world.

Despite these challenges, the NAM continues to offer significant opportunities for solidarity and cooperation among developing countries. The movement's emphasis on South-South cooperation, mutual support, and collective action provides a foundation for addressing shared challenges and advancing common interests. The NAM's commitment to peace, development, and justice remains a powerful force for positive change in international relations, providing a counterbalance to the dominance of powerful states and promoting a more inclusive and equitable world order.

The Non-Aligned Movement emerged as a powerful force in global politics during the Cold War, offering an alternative vision of international relations based on non-alignment, sovereignty, and solidarity. The movement provided a platform for newly independent states to assert their independence, promote their interests, and advocate for a more just and equitable international order. Through its emphasis on peaceful coexistence, economic justice, and South-South cooperation, the NAM played a critical role in shaping the global political landscape and advancing the interests of the Global South.

As we continue to explore the broader story of decolonization and the quest for self-determination, the Non-Aligned Movement offers valuable lessons on the complexities of building solidarity, promoting peace, and advocating for justice in a diverse and dynamic world. The movement's legacy continues to inspire and inform contemporary efforts to create a more inclusive, equitable, and peaceful international system.

Chapter 10: Economic Independence and Development Challenges

Introduction: The Struggle for Economic Independence in Newly Independent States

As newly independent states emerged from the shadow of colonialism in the mid-20th century, one of their most pressing challenges was achieving economic independence and sustainable development. For many of these countries, political sovereignty was only the first step; the next, and perhaps more difficult challenge, was to transform their economies from ones that had been structured to serve colonial interests to ones that could support self-sustaining growth and development. This chapter explores the economic policies pursued by leaders like Kwame Nkrumah in Ghana, Jawaharlal Nehru in India, and Ahmed Ben Bella in Algeria, and examines the role of international organizations such as the United Nations, the World Bank, and the International Monetary Fund (IMF) in shaping development outcomes. Through case studies of both success and failure, we will highlight the difficulties these countries faced in overcoming economic dependency, diversifying their economies, and achieving sustainable development.

Economic Policies in Newly Independent States: A Path to Self-Sufficiency?

Kwame Nkrumah and Ghana: A Vision of Industrialization and Pan-Africanism

Kwame Nkrumah, Ghana's first Prime Minister and later President, was a leading figure in the African independence movement and a staunch advocate for Pan-Africanism. Upon Ghana's independence in 1957, Nkrumah set out to transform the country's economy from one based on the export of primary commodities, particularly cocoa, to one that was more diversified and industrialized. He believed that economic independence was essential for true political independence and that African countries needed to unite and cooperate to break free from the neocolonial economic structures that kept them dependent on the former colonial powers.

Nkrumah's economic policies were heavily influenced by socialist principles and aimed at state-led industrialization. His government launched ambitious development plans, including the construction of the Akosombo Dam on the Volta River to generate hydroelectric power, the establishment of state-owned enterprises in various sectors such as manufacturing and mining, and investments in infrastructure, education, and healthcare. Nkrumah also promoted agricultural modernization to increase productivity and reduce dependency on cocoa exports.

However, Nkrumah's vision faced significant challenges. The heavy reliance on cocoa exports made Ghana vulnerable to fluctuations in world prices, and the ambitious industrialization projects required substantial foreign borrowing, leading to rising debt levels. The state-owned enterprises were often inefficient and plagued by corruption, and the rapid pace of economic transformation created social and political tensions. By 1966, economic difficulties, coupled with political unrest and dissatisfaction with Nkrumah's increasingly authoritarian rule, led to a military coup that overthrew his government. Ghana's experience under Nkrumah illustrates the difficulties of achieving economic independence and the complex interplay between political and economic factors in shaping development outcomes.

Jawaharlal Nehru and India: A Mixed Economy Approach

In India, Jawaharlal Nehru, the country's first Prime Minister, faced the enormous challenge of developing a diverse and populous nation emerging from nearly two centuries of British colonial rule. Nehru's economic vision was based on a mixed economy model, combining elements of socialism and capitalism. He believed in a strong role for the state in guiding economic development while also recognizing the importance of private enterprise.

Nehru's government implemented a series of five-year plans that prioritized industrialization, infrastructure development, and education. The public sector was expanded significantly, with state ownership of key industries such as steel, coal, and heavy machinery, as well as a focus on developing hydroelectric power and irrigation projects. Nehru's emphasis on scientific and technological development led to the establishment of premier institutions like the Indian Institutes of Technology (IITs) and the promotion of research in agriculture, leading to the Green Revolution in the 1960s and 1970s.

Despite these efforts, India's path to economic independence was fraught with challenges. The country faced persistent poverty, high population growth, and regional disparities in development. The reliance on state-led industrialization often led to inefficiencies and bureaucratic red tape, while the agricultural sector struggled with issues of land reform, productivity, and rural poverty. The mixed economy model also faced criticism for being too dependent on foreign aid and technology, particularly from the Soviet Union and the United States during the Cold War.

India's experience under Nehru reflects the complexities of achieving economic development in a large and diverse country. While the foundations for future growth were laid during Nehru's tenure, the country struggled to balance state intervention with market-driven policies and to address the deep-seated social and economic inequalities inherited from the colonial era.

Ahmed Ben Bella and Algeria: A Socialist Experiment in a Post-Colonial State

In Algeria, Ahmed Ben Bella, the country's first President after gaining independence from France in 1962, pursued a socialist path to economic development. Algeria's struggle for independence was one of the most violent and protracted of the decolonization era, and the new government faced the immense task of rebuilding a war-torn economy and society.

Ben Bella's economic policies were influenced by the socialist and anti-imperialist ideology that had shaped the Algerian independence movement. The government nationalized key sectors of the economy, including oil and gas, banking, and industry, and implemented land reform to redistribute land from European settlers to Algerian peasants. Ben Bella's government also sought to promote self-reliance and reduce dependency on foreign aid and imports by encouraging domestic production and industrialization.

However, Algeria's path to economic independence was marked by significant challenges. The nationalization of industries and the emphasis on state-led development often led to inefficiencies and a lack of productivity. The country's heavy reliance on oil and gas exports made it vulnerable to fluctuations in global energy prices, and the lack of diversification in the economy hindered long-term sustainable development. Political instability, coupled with internal divisions within the ruling party, led to Ben Bella's ouster in a coup in 1965, highlighting the difficulties of balancing economic transformation with political stability in a newly independent state.

The Role of International Organizations in Shaping Development Outcomes

United Nations and Development Aid

The United Nations (UN) played a significant role in supporting newly independent states in their efforts to achieve economic independence and development. Through various specialized agencies, such as the United Nations Development Programme (UNDP), the United Nations Conference on Trade and Development (UNCTAD), and the Food and Agriculture Organization (FAO), the UN provided technical assistance, capacity building, and financial support to help countries address development challenges.

The UN also served as a forum for newly independent states to articulate their interests and advocate for a more just and equitable international economic order. The NAM countries, in particular, used the UN platform to call for reforms in global trade, finance, and development assistance, promoting the principles of sovereignty, self-determination, and economic justice. The Group of 77 (G77), a coalition of developing countries formed within the UN, played a key role in advancing the agenda for a New International Economic Order (NIEO), which sought to address the structural inequalities in the global economic system and promote fair trade, technology transfer, and financial assistance to developing countries.

The World Bank and International Monetary Fund: Balancing Development and Debt

The World Bank and the International Monetary Fund (IMF) were also pivotal in shaping development outcomes in newly independent states. These institutions provided financial assistance, technical expertise, and policy advice to help countries stabilize their economies, build infrastructure, and promote economic growth. However, their role in developing countries has been a subject of significant debate and controversy.

The World Bank, initially focused on rebuilding war-torn Europe, shifted its attention to development finance in the Global South in the 1950s and 1960s. It provided loans for infrastructure projects, such as dams, roads, and power plants, which were seen as critical for fostering economic growth and development. However, the conditions attached to these loans often emphasized market-oriented reforms, privatization, and liberalization, which sometimes clashed with the developmental priorities of the borrowing countries.

The IMF, primarily concerned with macroeconomic stability, provided short-term financial assistance to countries facing balance of payments crises. However, the IMF's structural adjustment programs (SAPs) in the 1980s and 1990s, which required countries to implement austerity measures, reduce public spending, and liberalize their economies, were criticized for exacerbating poverty and inequality and undermining social welfare programs.

The reliance on World Bank and IMF loans often led to a cycle of debt dependency, as countries struggled to repay their loans while implementing the required economic reforms. The debt crisis of the 1980s, particularly in Latin America and Africa, highlighted the difficulties of achieving economic independence in the face of global economic pressures and the limitations of the development model promoted by these institutions.

Case Studies of Success and Failure: Lessons from the Global South

Success Story: The "Asian Tigers" and Export-Oriented Industrialization

While many newly independent states struggled to achieve economic independence and sustainable development, some countries in Asia, known as the "Asian Tigers"—South Korea, Taiwan, Singapore, and Hong Kong—achieved remarkable economic success through export-oriented industrialization (EOI). These countries adopted strategies that focused on developing competitive export industries, investing in human capital, and maintaining macroeconomic stability.

South Korea and Taiwan, in particular, pursued state-led industrialization policies that combined government intervention with market-oriented reforms. The governments provided subsidies, credit, and technical support to promote export industries, such as textiles, electronics, and automobiles, while also investing heavily in education, infrastructure, and technology development. These countries also maintained high levels of savings and investment, ensuring that the gains from economic growth were reinvested in further development.

The success of the Asian Tigers highlights the importance of strategic economic planning, investment in human capital, and the ability to adapt to global market conditions. It also underscores the potential for newly independent states to achieve economic independence and development by leveraging their comparative advantages, building strong institutions, and fostering a favorable investment climate.

Failure to Thrive: The Case of Zambia and the Resource Curse

Zambia, a landlocked country in Southern Africa, provides a contrasting example of the challenges faced by newly independent states in achieving sustainable development. At independence in 1964, Zambia was one of the most prosperous countries in Africa, thanks to its vast copper reserves. However, the country's heavy reliance on copper exports made it vulnerable to fluctuations in global commodity prices, leading to economic instability and decline.

The Zambian government, under President Kenneth Kaunda, initially pursued a policy of nationalization and state-led development, taking control of the copper mines and other key sectors of the economy. However, the nationalized industries were often inefficient and plagued by corruption and mismanagement. The collapse of copper prices in the 1970s and 1980s, coupled with rising debt levels and declining foreign exchange reserves, plunged Zambia into a deep economic crisis.

The IMF and World Bank imposed structural adjustment programs in the 1980s, requiring Zambia to implement austerity measures, liberalize its economy, and privatize state-owned enterprises. These policies led to social and economic hardships, including increased poverty, unemployment, and social unrest. The experience of Zambia underscores the challenges of achieving economic independence in the face of global economic pressures, the limitations of reliance on primary commodities, and the difficulties of balancing state intervention with market-oriented reforms.

Overcoming Economic Dependency: Strategies for Sustainable Development

Diversification and Industrialization: Building Resilient Economies

One of the key challenges for newly independent states in achieving economic independence is overcoming economic dependency on a narrow range of exports and developing more diversified and resilient economies. Diversification and industrialization are critical strategies for reducing vulnerability to external shocks, creating jobs, and fostering sustainable growth.

Countries that have successfully diversified their economies have often invested in human capital, infrastructure, and technology development, promoting innovation and competitiveness in a range of sectors. The experiences of countries like Malaysia, which transitioned from a primary commodity exporter to a diversified industrial economy, highlight the importance of strategic economic planning, investment in education and skills development, and fostering a conducive environment for private sector growth.

Promoting Inclusive Growth and Reducing Inequality

Achieving sustainable development also requires addressing the social and economic inequalities that often persist in newly independent states. Inclusive growth strategies, which focus on ensuring that the benefits of economic growth are broadly shared, are essential for promoting social cohesion, reducing poverty, and fostering long-term stability.

Policies that promote inclusive growth may include targeted social programs, such as cash transfers, public works, and social insurance, as well as investments in health, education, and rural development. Land reform, access to credit, and support for small and medium-sized enterprises (SMEs) are also important for promoting inclusive economic opportunities and reducing inequality.

Strengthening Institutions and Governance

Strong institutions and good governance are critical for achieving sustainable development and overcoming economic dependency. Effective governance requires transparent and accountable institutions, the rule of law, and the capacity to implement sound economic policies. Countries with strong institutions are better able to manage economic shocks, attract investment, and promote development.

Strengthening institutions and governance involves building the capacity of public administration, improving regulatory frameworks, combating corruption, and fostering inclusive political processes. The experiences of countries like Botswana, which has maintained strong institutions and good governance while achieving sustained economic growth, underscore the importance of these factors in achieving long-term development success.

The struggle for economic independence and sustainable development has been a central challenge for newly independent states in the postcolonial era. While many countries have made significant progress in transforming their economies and reducing dependency on former colonial powers, the path to development has been fraught with difficulties, including economic volatility, external pressures, and internal governance challenges.

The experiences of leaders like Kwame Nkrumah, Jawaharlal Nehru, and Ahmed Ben Bella, as well as the role of international organizations such as the United Nations, the World Bank, and the IMF, provide valuable lessons on the complexities of achieving economic independence in a globalized world. The successes and failures of different countries highlight the importance of strategic economic planning, diversification, inclusive growth, and strong institutions in overcoming economic dependency and fostering sustainable development.

Chapter 11: Cultural Reawakening and Postcolonial Identity

Introduction: Rediscovering Identity in a Postcolonial World

The end of colonial rule in Asia, Africa, and the Caribbean was not just a political and economic transition but also a profound cultural transformation. Newly independent nations faced the challenge of forging new national identities that could unite diverse populations and reflect their unique histories and aspirations. In this context, a cultural reawakening emerged across the postcolonial world, marked by a resurgence of indigenous cultures, languages, and traditions, and the rise of powerful literary and artistic movements. This chapter explores the cultural reawakening and search for postcolonial identity in Asia, Africa, and the Caribbean, highlighting significant movements such as Negritude in Africa and the Caribbean Renaissance. We will examine how these movements challenged colonial narratives, celebrated indigenous heritage, and helped shape the national identities of newly independent states.

The Resurgence of Indigenous Cultures, Languages, and Traditions

Reclaiming Cultural Heritage: A Rejection of Colonial Hegemony

Colonial rule often sought to suppress or marginalize indigenous cultures, languages, and traditions, promoting instead the languages, religions, and cultural practices of the colonizers. In the aftermath of independence, many newly independent states embarked on a process of cultural reawakening, seeking to reclaim and revitalize their indigenous cultural heritage. This resurgence was seen as essential to rebuilding a sense of national identity, pride, and unity in the postcolonial context.

In Africa, the process of cultural reclamation often involved reviving traditional arts, music, dance, and oral literature that had been suppressed or devalued during colonial rule. Many African countries adopted policies that promoted the use of indigenous languages in education, government, and media, seeking to reverse the linguistic and cultural domination of the colonial period. For example, in Tanzania, President Julius Nyerere promoted the use of Kiswahili as a national language, uniting diverse ethnic groups and fostering a sense of national identity.

Similarly, in Asia, countries like India, Indonesia, and Vietnam sought to revive and promote their cultural heritage as a means of asserting their sovereignty and independence. In India, the revival of classical music, dance, and literature, along with the promotion of regional languages, became central to the project of nation-building and cultural renaissance. In Indonesia, the promotion of Bahasa Indonesia as the national language and the celebration of traditional arts and crafts were integral to the post-independence cultural policy.

In the Caribbean, the reclamation of cultural heritage often involved a complex negotiation of multiple influences, including African, indigenous, and European traditions. The celebration of

Afro-Caribbean culture, including music genres like reggae and calypso, religious practices like Rastafarianism and Vodou, and festivals like Carnival, became central to the Caribbean cultural identity. This cultural revival was seen as a rejection of colonial domination and a reaffirmation of the region's diverse cultural roots.

Revitalizing Indigenous Languages: A Key to Cultural Identity

Language has always been a powerful tool of cultural expression and identity. In the postcolonial era, the promotion and revitalization of indigenous languages became a critical aspect of cultural reawakening. Many newly independent states recognized that the preservation and promotion of indigenous languages were essential for maintaining cultural diversity and ensuring that future generations could connect with their cultural heritage.

In Africa, the promotion of indigenous languages was seen as a way to break free from the linguistic dominance of colonial languages like English, French, and Portuguese. Countries such as Tanzania, Kenya, and Nigeria implemented policies to promote indigenous languages in schools and government institutions. In South Africa, the post-apartheid government recognized 11 official languages, reflecting the country's commitment to linguistic diversity and cultural inclusion.

In Asia, countries like India adopted a multilingual policy, recognizing both Hindi and English as official languages while also promoting regional languages. In the Philippines, efforts were made to promote Filipino, based on Tagalog, as a national language, alongside English. Similarly, in Malaysia, the promotion of Malay as a national language was seen as a means of fostering national unity and cultural pride.

In the Caribbean, the promotion of Creole languages, such as Haitian Creole and Jamaican Patois, became an important aspect of cultural reawakening. These languages, often marginalized during colonial rule, were celebrated as expressions of the region's unique cultural identity, blending African, European, and indigenous influences. The recognition and promotion of Creole languages were seen as acts of cultural defiance against the colonial legacy and as affirmations of the region's diverse cultural heritage.

Significant Literary and Artistic Movements: Challenging Colonial Narratives

Negritude: Reclaiming African Identity and Dignity

One of the most influential literary and cultural movements to emerge in the postcolonial era was Negritude, a movement that sought to reclaim African identity, culture, and dignity in the face of colonial oppression. Negritude was founded in the 1930s by a group of African and Caribbean intellectuals, including Aimé Césaire from Martinique, Léopold Sédar Senghor from Senegal, and Léon Damas from French Guiana, who were studying in Paris at the time.

Negritude emerged as a response to the dehumanizing effects of colonialism and racism, which sought to deny the humanity and culture of African peoples. The movement sought to celebrate the beauty, richness, and diversity of African cultures and to challenge the stereotypes and prejudices propagated by colonialism. Through poetry, literature, and essays, the proponents of Negritude articulated a vision of African identity that was rooted in a shared cultural heritage and a sense of pride in being Black.

Léopold Sédar Senghor, one of the leading figures of Negritude, emphasized the importance of reclaiming African cultural values and aesthetics as a means of resisting colonial domination and fostering a sense of national pride. His poetry celebrated the rhythms, myths, and symbols of African culture, while his essays called for a re-evaluation of African identity in the context of a postcolonial world. Senghor's ideas had a profound influence on the cultural policies of newly independent African states, particularly in his home country of Senegal, where he served as the first President.

Aimé Césaire, another key figure of Negritude, used his poetry and plays to critique colonialism and advocate for the cultural and political emancipation of African and Caribbean peoples. His seminal work, "Cahier d'un retour au pays natal" (Notebook of a Return to the Native Land), became a manifesto for the Negritude movement, blending poetic imagery with political critique to explore themes of identity, exile, and resistance.

Negritude played a crucial role in shaping the cultural and political discourse of postcolonial Africa and the Caribbean, inspiring generations of writers, artists, and intellectuals to explore and celebrate their cultural heritage and to challenge the legacies of colonialism.

Caribbean Renaissance: A Cultural Revival of Diversity and Resistance

In the Caribbean, the search for postcolonial identity was shaped by the region's complex history of colonization, slavery, and cultural hybridity. The Caribbean Renaissance, a cultural and literary movement that emerged in the mid-20th century, sought to articulate a new cultural identity that reflected the region's diverse heritage and complex social realities.

The Caribbean Renaissance was characterized by a revival of interest in the region's Afro-Caribbean culture, folklore, and oral traditions, as well as a critique of the colonial legacy and its impact on Caribbean societies. Writers, poets, and artists from the region sought to reclaim their cultural heritage and express their unique voices in the face of cultural domination by colonial powers.

One of the most influential figures of the Caribbean Renaissance was Derek Walcott, a Nobel Prize-winning poet and playwright from Saint Lucia. Walcott's work explored themes of identity, exile, and cultural hybridity, reflecting the complex cultural landscape of the Caribbean. His poetry celebrated the region's diverse cultural heritage while also grappling with the legacies of colonialism and slavery. Walcott's play "Dream on Monkey Mountain" is a powerful exploration of identity, colonialism, and the search for self in a postcolonial context.

Another significant figure was Edward Kamau Brathwaite, a Barbadian poet and scholar whose work focused on the cultural and historical experiences of Afro-Caribbean peoples. Brathwaite's poetry, including his famous trilogy "The Arrivants," sought to capture the rhythms and language of the Caribbean, blending African, European, and indigenous influences. He was also a leading advocate for the use of Creole languages in literature and a critic of the cultural imperialism that sought to marginalize Afro-Caribbean culture.

The Caribbean Renaissance also encompassed the visual arts, music, and theater, with artists and musicians drawing on indigenous, African, and European traditions to create new forms of cultural expression. The revival of Carnival and other traditional festivals, as well as the rise of music genres like reggae, calypso, and salsa, became powerful expressions of cultural identity and resistance to colonial legacies.

Challenging Colonial Narratives and Shaping National Identities

Decolonizing the Mind: Intellectual Movements and Cultural Critique

One of the central goals of the cultural reawakening in the postcolonial world was to challenge and deconstruct the colonial narratives that had shaped perceptions of colonized peoples and their cultures. Colonialism had not only imposed political and economic domination but had also sought to impose cultural and intellectual hegemony, often portraying colonized peoples as backward, inferior, and incapable of self-governance.

In response, intellectual movements and cultural critics from across Asia, Africa, and the Caribbean sought to "decolonize the mind" by challenging these narratives and asserting the value and dignity of indigenous cultures and identities. In his seminal work, "The Wretched of the Earth," Frantz Fanon, a Martinican psychiatrist and revolutionary, argued that decolonization must be a total process, encompassing not only political and economic liberation but also the reclamation of cultural and psychological autonomy.

Fanon's work, along with that of other intellectuals such as Ngũgĩ wa Thiong'o, Amilcar Cabral, and Albert Memmi, emphasized the importance of cultural liberation as a means of resisting colonial domination and building a new national consciousness. Ngũgĩ wa Thiong'o, a Kenyan writer and scholar, famously advocated for writing in indigenous languages as a way to resist cultural imperialism and reconnect with African cultural roots. His works, such as "Decolonising the Mind," called for a radical rethinking of cultural production and education in postcolonial societies.

These intellectual movements played a crucial role in shaping national identities in the postcolonial era, emphasizing the importance of cultural pride, historical consciousness, and resistance to cultural domination. They provided a framework for understanding the cultural dimensions of decolonization and the ongoing struggle for self-determination and sovereignty.

National Culture and Postcolonial State-Building

The cultural reawakening in the postcolonial world was closely linked to the process of state-building and nation-building. Newly independent states sought to forge a sense of national identity and unity that could transcend ethnic, linguistic, and religious differences. National culture was seen as a critical element of this project, providing a common foundation upon which to build a new national consciousness and sense of belonging.

In many postcolonial states, cultural policies were developed to promote national unity and identity, often through the revival and promotion of indigenous cultures, languages, and traditions. These policies were often accompanied by efforts to create new national symbols, such as flags, anthems, and public holidays that could serve as unifying symbols of national identity.

In Senegal, for example, President Léopold Sédar Senghor, a leading figure of the Negritude movement, placed a strong emphasis on cultural policy as a means of nation-building. Senghor sought to promote a sense of national identity based on a synthesis of African cultural values and modern development goals. His government invested in cultural institutions, such as museums, theaters, and art schools, and promoted Senegalese literature, music, and dance as expressions of national identity.

Similarly, in India, cultural policy under Prime Minister Jawaharlal Nehru sought to promote a sense of national unity and pride in India's diverse cultural heritage. Nehru emphasized the importance of secularism, democracy, and cultural pluralism as foundational principles of the Indian state and promoted the celebration of India's rich cultural diversity through festivals, museums, and cultural exchanges.

In the Caribbean, cultural policy often focused on reclaiming and celebrating the region's Afro-Caribbean heritage and promoting cultural diversity as a source of strength and identity. Governments invested in cultural institutions, such as the University of the West Indies, and promoted the use of Creole languages, music, and festivals as expressions of national identity.

The Impact of Cultural Reawakening on Postcolonial Societies Reclaiming Dignity and Empowerment

The cultural reawakening in the postcolonial world had a profound impact on the societies emerging from the shadow of colonial rule. By reclaiming their cultural heritage, languages, and traditions, newly independent states sought to assert their sovereignty, dignity, and identity in a global context that had long marginalized and devalued them. The cultural revival provided a source of pride and empowerment for many communities, fostering a sense of belonging and unity in the face of ongoing challenges.

The celebration of indigenous cultures and the rejection of colonial narratives also helped to build a sense of historical consciousness and continuity, reconnecting people with their pre-colonial pasts and affirming their cultural identities. This process was particularly important in societies that had been subjected to cultural erasure and dehumanization under colonial rule, providing a foundation for the construction of new national narratives and identities.

Challenges of Cultural Revival and Identity Formation

Despite the positive impact of cultural reawakening, the process of reclaiming and reshaping postcolonial identities was not without challenges. In many cases, the revival of indigenous cultures and traditions was accompanied by debates over the meanings and interpretations of cultural heritage, the role of traditional practices in modern society, and the tensions between cultural revival and modernization.

In some cases, efforts to promote national culture and identity were criticized for being overly prescriptive or exclusionary, privileging certain cultural narratives or practices over others. This was particularly evident in multicultural societies, where the promotion of a single national culture sometimes marginalized or excluded minority cultures and identities. Balancing the promotion of national unity with the recognition and celebration of cultural diversity remains a key challenge for many postcolonial states.

Additionally, the process of cultural revival was often complicated by the legacies of colonialism and the ongoing influence of global cultural and economic forces. The penetration of global media, consumer culture, and economic globalization has continued to shape cultural production and consumption in postcolonial societies, sometimes challenging efforts to promote indigenous cultures and traditions.

The cultural reawakening in the postcolonial world was a powerful response to the legacies of colonialism and a critical aspect of the broader struggle for independence and self-determination. Through the resurgence of indigenous cultures, languages, and traditions, and the rise of significant literary and artistic movements, newly independent states sought to reclaim their cultural heritage, challenge colonial narratives, and forge new national identities.

Movements like Negritude in Africa and the Caribbean Renaissance played a central role in this process, celebrating cultural diversity, resisting cultural domination, and articulating new visions of postcolonial identity. These movements not only shaped national cultures and identities but also contributed to a broader global dialogue on decolonization, cultural resistance, and the quest for dignity and empowerment.

Chapter 12: Conflicts and Continuity in Postcolonial States

Introduction: The Legacy of Colonial Borders and Ethnic Divisions

The end of colonial rule in Asia, Africa, and the Caribbean brought about not only independence and sovereignty but also a host of challenges that many newly independent states were ill-equipped to handle. One of the most enduring and destabilizing legacies of colonialism has been the arbitrary borders drawn by colonial powers, which often ignored ethnic, cultural, and religious boundaries. These borders, along with the colonial strategy of divide-and-rule, sowed the seeds for internal conflicts and civil wars in many postcolonial states. This chapter explores the conflicts and continuity in postcolonial states, focusing on how colonial borders and ethnic divisions have led to internal strife in countries such as Nigeria, Sudan, and the Indian subcontinent. We will analyze the role of foreign intervention, Cold War geopolitics, and local power struggles in these conflicts and reflect on the challenges of nation-building and governance in diverse societies.

Colonial Legacies and Internal Conflicts: A Troubled Inheritance

The Creation of Artificial Borders: Igniting Ethnic Tensions

Colonial powers, in their quest for control and exploitation, often drew arbitrary borders that paid little attention to the ethnic, cultural, and historical realities of the regions they colonized. These artificial borders frequently grouped together diverse and sometimes antagonistic ethnic and religious groups, while splitting apart communities that shared common identities and histories. The result was a patchwork of multi-ethnic states with little sense of national unity or cohesion, setting the stage for postcolonial conflicts.

In Africa, the Berlin Conference of 1884-1885, where European powers divided the continent into spheres of influence, is a prime example of the disregard for indigenous political and cultural boundaries. The imposition of these artificial borders often forced diverse groups into uneasy coexistence within the same state, leading to competition for resources, political power, and cultural dominance. This situation was further exacerbated by the colonial practice of favoring certain ethnic groups over others, creating hierarchies of privilege and resentment that persisted into the postcolonial era.

In Asia, the partition of India in 1947, which led to the creation of the separate states of India and Pakistan, is another example of the lasting impact of colonial borders. The division was based on religious lines, with predominantly Muslim regions forming Pakistan and predominantly Hindu regions forming India. However, the hastily drawn borders left millions of people on the "wrong" side, leading to one of the largest mass migrations in history and widespread violence between Hindus, Muslims, and Sikhs. The partition also laid the groundwork for future conflicts between India and Pakistan, including three wars and ongoing disputes over the Kashmir region.

Divide and Rule: Colonial Policies and Ethnic Fragmentation

Colonial powers often employed a strategy of divide-and-rule, exploiting ethnic, religious, and social divisions to maintain control over their colonies. By favoring certain groups over others and fostering divisions among the colonized populations, colonial rulers sought to prevent unified resistance against their rule. This policy had a lasting impact on postcolonial states, where ethnic and religious tensions, fueled by colonial favoritism and competition for power, often erupted into violence.

In Nigeria, British colonial rule exacerbated existing ethnic divisions by favoring certain ethnic groups, such as the Hausa-Fulani in the north and the Yoruba in the southwest, while marginalizing others, such as the Igbo in the southeast. This created a legacy of ethnic competition and mistrust that would later contribute to Nigeria's brutal civil war, known as the Biafran War, in the late 1960s.

Similarly, in Sudan, British colonial rule deepened divisions between the predominantly Arab and Muslim north and the largely African and Christian or animist south. The colonial administration's policies of indirect rule, which favored northern elites and marginalized southern communities, created a legacy of distrust and resentment that would fuel decades of civil conflict after independence in 1956.

Case Studies of Conflict: Nigeria, Sudan, and the Indian Subcontinent

Nigeria: The Biafran War and Ethnic Tensions

Nigeria, Africa's most populous country, is a microcosm of the continent's ethnic diversity and colonial legacy. With over 250 ethnic groups and significant regional, religious, and cultural differences, Nigeria faced significant challenges in building a cohesive national identity after gaining independence from Britain in 1960. The tensions between the three major ethnic groups—the Hausa-Fulani in the north, the Yoruba in the southwest, and the Igbo in the southeast—were exacerbated by colonial policies that favored different groups in different regions.

The immediate post-independence period was marked by political instability, regional rivalries, and ethnic tensions, which culminated in a series of military coups. The most significant conflict was the Biafran War, also known as the Nigerian Civil War, which erupted in 1967 when the southeastern region, dominated by the Igbo ethnic group, declared independence as the Republic of Biafra. The war was fueled by a combination of ethnic tensions, political grievances, and competition for control over the country's oil-rich regions.

The Nigerian government, determined to maintain national unity, launched a military campaign to suppress the Biafran secession. The war lasted for three years and resulted in widespread devastation, including a humanitarian crisis marked by mass starvation and displacement. Estimates of the death toll range from one to three million people, making it one of the deadliest conflicts in postcolonial Africa.

The Biafran War highlighted the deep-seated ethnic divisions and challenges of nation-building in Nigeria. While the war ended with Biafra's reintegration into Nigeria in 1970, the underlying ethnic and regional tensions have persisted, contributing to ongoing political instability, violence, and underdevelopment.

Sudan: Civil Wars and the Struggle for Unity

Sudan, Africa's largest country until the secession of South Sudan in 2011, has been plagued by internal conflicts and civil wars since gaining independence from Britain and Egypt in 1956. The country's diverse population, divided along ethnic, religious, and cultural lines, has faced significant challenges in building a cohesive national identity.

The First Sudanese Civil War (1955-1972) erupted shortly before independence, as southern Sudanese groups, feeling marginalized and excluded from political power, took up arms against the northern-dominated government. The war was fueled by a combination of ethnic, religious, and economic grievances, with the southern rebels seeking greater autonomy and recognition of their cultural and religious rights.

The Addis Ababa Agreement in 1972 brought a temporary end to the conflict by granting the south limited autonomy. However, tensions resurfaced in the early 1980s, leading to the outbreak of the Second Sudanese Civil War (1983-2005). The conflict was triggered by the government's imposition of Islamic law (Sharia) and the abrogation of the Addis Ababa Agreement, which reignited southern grievances. The war was characterized by widespread atrocities, including ethnic cleansing, mass displacement, and famine, resulting in the deaths of an estimated two million people.

The Comprehensive Peace Agreement (CPA) in 2005 marked the end of the Second Civil War and paved the way for a referendum on southern independence. In 2011, South Sudan voted overwhelmingly for independence, becoming the world's newest nation. However, the secession did not bring peace to the region. Both Sudan and South Sudan have continued to face internal conflicts, fueled by ethnic rivalries, economic competition, and political power struggles.

Sudan's conflicts reflect the deep-seated divisions and challenges of nation-building in a diverse society with a complex colonial history. The struggle for unity and stability in Sudan and South Sudan remains an ongoing challenge, highlighting the difficulties of overcoming the legacies of colonialism and achieving inclusive governance and development.

The Indian Subcontinent: Partition and Persistent Rivalries

The partition of British India in 1947 into the separate states of India and Pakistan remains one of the most traumatic events in the region's history, with lasting implications for both countries. The partition was based on religious lines, with predominantly Muslim regions forming Pakistan (including East Pakistan, which later became Bangladesh) and predominantly Hindu regions forming India. The division was accompanied by widespread violence, mass displacement, and communal riots, resulting in the deaths of an estimated one to two million people and the displacement of over 15 million.

The partition left a legacy of deep-seated animosity and mistrust between India and Pakistan, leading to a series of conflicts and wars. The two countries fought three major wars (in 1947-1948, 1965, and 1971) and several smaller skirmishes, primarily over the disputed region of Kashmir, which remains a flashpoint for conflict to this day. The 1971 war resulted in the independence of East Pakistan as Bangladesh, adding another layer of complexity to the region's political landscape.

The conflicts between India and Pakistan have been shaped not only by historical grievances and territorial disputes but also by broader geopolitical dynamics, including Cold War rivalries and the nuclear arms race. Both countries have pursued nuclear weapons programs, further escalating tensions and increasing the risks of a potentially catastrophic conflict.

The Indian subcontinent's experience with partition and persistent conflicts underscores the challenges of building cohesive national identities and achieving stable governance in a region marked by religious, ethnic, and cultural diversity. The ongoing disputes over Kashmir and other issues continue to pose significant challenges to peace and stability in the region.

Foreign Intervention, Cold War Geopolitics, and Local Power Struggles

The Role of Foreign Intervention: Fueling Conflicts and Proxy Wars

The Cold War era saw significant foreign intervention in the internal affairs of postcolonial states, as the United States and the Soviet Union sought to expand their influence and contain each other's power. Many postcolonial conflicts became arenas for proxy wars, where local power struggles were exacerbated by the involvement of external powers.

In Africa, the Angolan Civil War (1975-2002) became a classic example of a Cold War proxy conflict, with the United States and its allies supporting one faction, while the Soviet Union and Cuba supported another. Similarly, in the Horn of Africa, the Ogaden War between Ethiopia and Somalia (1977-1978) saw both superpowers providing military support to opposing sides, further complicating the conflict and prolonging regional instability.

In the Middle East, foreign intervention has played a significant role in shaping postcolonial conflicts. The Iranian Revolution of 1979 and the subsequent Iran-Iraq War (1980-1988) saw significant foreign involvement, with the United States, the Soviet Union, and other regional powers providing support to different sides. The Israeli-Palestinian conflict, rooted in the partition of Palestine and the creation of the state of Israel in 1948, has also been shaped by foreign intervention, including U.S. military and financial support for Israel and support for Palestinian groups by various Arab states.

Foreign intervention has often exacerbated local conflicts, increasing their intensity and duration and complicating efforts to achieve peace and stability. The involvement of external powers has also sometimes undermined the sovereignty and autonomy of postcolonial states, making it difficult for them to resolve their internal conflicts on their own terms.

Cold War Geopolitics: Ideological Rivalries and Regional Alliances

The Cold War rivalry between the United States and the Soviet Union had a profound impact on postcolonial states, as newly independent countries were often drawn into the global struggle between capitalism and communism. Many postcolonial leaders sought to navigate this complex landscape by adopting policies of non-alignment, seeking to avoid becoming pawns in the superpower rivalry.

However, the pressures of the Cold War often made non-alignment difficult to maintain. In many cases, local conflicts were influenced or exacerbated by the ideological competition between the superpowers. In Southeast Asia, the Vietnam War (1955-1975) became a major Cold War conflict, with the United States intervening to prevent the spread of communism and the Soviet Union and China supporting the communist North Vietnamese forces.

In Latin America, the Cuban Revolution of 1959 and the subsequent U.S. efforts to contain the spread of socialism in the region led to a series of conflicts and interventions, including the Bay of Pigs invasion, the Cuban Missile Crisis, and U.S. support for anti-communist regimes and insurgencies throughout the region. The Cold War dynamics often led to the entrenchment of authoritarian regimes, as both superpowers were willing to support dictatorships that aligned with their strategic interests.

The influence of Cold War geopolitics on postcolonial conflicts underscores the challenges of nation-building and governance in a world shaped by ideological rivalries and external pressures. The legacies of these Cold War conflicts continue to affect the political landscapes of many postcolonial states, contributing to ongoing instability and unrest.

Local Power Struggles: The Challenge of Governance in Diverse Societies

In addition to foreign intervention and Cold War geopolitics, local power struggles have also played a significant role in shaping conflicts and continuity in postcolonial states. Many newly independent states faced the challenge of building cohesive national identities and inclusive political systems in societies marked by ethnic, religious, and cultural diversity.

In some cases, local power struggles have been fueled by competition for control over resources, political power, and economic opportunities. In Nigeria, for example, the discovery of oil in the Niger Delta region has been both a blessing and a curse, providing significant revenues for the government but also fueling conflicts over control of the region's resources. Militants in the Niger Delta have waged an insurgency against the government, demanding a greater share of the oil wealth and environmental justice for the region's communities.

In other cases, local power struggles have been shaped by historical grievances, social inequalities, and the legacies of colonial rule. In Kenya, the Mau Mau Uprising (1952-1960) against British colonial rule was fueled by land grievances and ethnic tensions between the Kikuyu and other communities. The post-independence period has seen continued tensions over land ownership, political power, and ethnic representation, contributing to periodic outbreaks of violence, including the post-election violence in 2007-2008.

The challenge of governance in diverse societies is compounded by issues of corruption, weak institutions, and a lack of inclusive political processes. In many postcolonial states, the concentration of power in the hands of a single ethnic or political group has led to exclusion, marginalization, and resentment, fueling internal conflicts and undermining efforts at nation-building.

Challenges of Nation-Building and Governance in Postcolonial States

Building Inclusive Political Systems: The Quest for National Unity

One of the central challenges of nation-building in postcolonial states is the need to build inclusive political systems that can accommodate diverse ethnic, religious, and cultural identities. The failure to do so has often resulted in internal conflicts, civil wars, and political instability.

Many postcolonial states have struggled to find the right balance between unity and diversity, centralization and decentralization, and inclusion and exclusion. In some cases, efforts to promote national unity have been perceived as attempts to impose the dominance of one group over others, leading to resistance and conflict. In other cases, the lack of inclusive political processes has resulted in the marginalization of certain groups and the entrenchment of ethnic and regional rivalries.

The experiences of countries like India, South Africa, and Indonesia offer valuable lessons on the importance of inclusive governance in diverse societies. India's commitment to democratic governance, secularism, and cultural pluralism has helped to manage its vast diversity and build a sense of national unity, despite ongoing challenges. South Africa's transition from apartheid to democracy, marked by a commitment to reconciliation, inclusion, and social justice, has provided a model for managing diversity in a postcolonial context.

Addressing Historical Grievances and Social Inequalities

Another key challenge of nation-building in postcolonial states is the need to address historical grievances and social inequalities that have often been exacerbated by colonial rule. The legacies of colonialism, including land dispossession, economic exploitation, and social hierarchies, continue to shape the political and economic landscapes of many postcolonial states.

Efforts to address these grievances and promote social justice have often been complicated by political resistance, economic constraints, and social divisions. Land reform, for example, has been a contentious issue in many postcolonial states, with efforts to redistribute land often encountering opposition from powerful elites and resistance from marginalized communities.

Addressing social inequalities also requires a commitment to inclusive economic development, investment in education and healthcare, and the promotion of social cohesion. In many postcolonial states, however, economic policies have often been shaped by external pressures, including debt, structural adjustment programs, and global market forces, which have sometimes undermined efforts to promote inclusive development and social justice.

Promoting Peace and Stability in a Multipolar World

The post-Cold War era has brought new challenges and opportunities for postcolonial states seeking to promote peace and stability in a multipolar world. The end of the Cold War has reduced the influence of superpower rivalry on internal conflicts, but it has also created new dynamics and challenges, including regional conflicts, terrorism, and the rise of new powers.

Postcolonial states must navigate a complex and evolving international landscape, balancing their interests and sovereignty with the demands of a globalized world. The experiences of countries like Rwanda, Sierra Leone, and Liberia, which have emerged from devastating conflicts to build more inclusive and stable societies, provide valuable lessons on the importance of reconciliation, institutional reform, and regional cooperation in promoting peace and stability.

The conflicts and continuity in postcolonial states reflect the complex legacies of colonialism, the challenges of nation-building in diverse societies, and the interplay of local and global dynamics in shaping postcolonial governance. The arbitrary borders and ethnic divisions inherited from colonial rule, coupled with the legacies of divide-and-rule policies, have often fueled internal conflicts and civil wars, complicating efforts to build cohesive and inclusive national identities.

The role of foreign intervention, Cold War geopolitics, and local power struggles in these conflicts underscores the challenges of achieving sovereignty and self-determination in a globalized world. The experiences of countries like Nigeria, Sudan, and the Indian subcontinent highlight the difficulties of overcoming historical grievances, promoting inclusive governance, and achieving peace and stability in diverse societies.

Chapter 13: Decolonization's Impact on Modern International Relations

Introduction: Decolonization and the Transformation of Global Order

Decolonization, the process through which countries in Asia, Africa, the Middle East, and the Caribbean gained independence from colonial powers, fundamentally reshaped the global order in the 20th century. The emergence of dozens of new states from the former colonies dramatically altered the landscape of international relations, introducing new voices, perspectives, and demands for justice, equality, and sovereignty. As these newly independent states joined the international community, they began to assert their influence through participation in international organizations, regional alliances, and global forums. This chapter explores the impact of decolonization on modern international relations, highlighting how former colonies have shaped contemporary geopolitics, the ongoing struggles for autonomy and independence in regions like Palestine and Western Sahara, and the rise of emerging economies from the Global South. We will reflect on how these developments have influenced global power dynamics and contributed to a more multipolar world order.

Former Colonies in the International Arena: Shaping Global Governance

The United Nations: A Platform for the Newly Independent States

The United Nations (UN), founded in 1945 in the aftermath of World War II, provided a crucial platform for newly independent states to assert their sovereignty and engage in global governance. As decolonization accelerated in the mid-20th century, the UN General Assembly expanded rapidly, with many newly independent countries from Africa, Asia, and the Caribbean joining the organization. By the 1960s and 1970s, the majority of UN member states were from the Global South, giving these countries significant influence in shaping the agenda and policies of the organization.

The newly independent states used the UN as a forum to advocate for decolonization, disarmament, economic justice, and human rights. The General Assembly became a critical arena for debates on self-determination, racial equality, and anti-colonial struggles. The Group of 77 (G77), a coalition of developing countries established in 1964, became a powerful bloc within the UN, advocating for a New International Economic Order (NIEO) that would address the structural inequalities in the global economic system and promote fair trade, development assistance, and technology transfer.

The UN's role in decolonization was also reflected in its support for the self-determination of peoples still under colonial rule. The adoption of the Declaration on the Granting of Independence to Colonial Countries and Peoples in 1960 was a landmark moment, reaffirming the UN's commitment to decolonization and the rights of all peoples to self-determination. The UN's Special Committee on Decolonization, also known as the Committee of 24, was established to monitor the process of decolonization and support the efforts of territories seeking independence.

Through their participation in the UN, newly independent states helped to shape global norms and principles related to sovereignty, human rights, and economic justice. The influence of the Global South within the UN has continued to be significant, as these countries advocate for reforms in global governance, greater representation, and a more equitable international order.

Regional Alliances and Groupings: Building Solidarity and Cooperation

In addition to their participation in the UN, newly independent states also sought to build regional alliances and groupings to promote solidarity, cooperation, and mutual support. These regional organizations became important platforms for addressing common challenges, fostering economic integration, and asserting collective interests in global affairs.

In Africa, the Organization of African Unity (OAU), established in 1963, provided a forum for African countries to coordinate their policies on decolonization, economic development, and political integration. The OAU played a significant role in supporting liberation movements across the continent, including in Angola, Mozambique, Namibia, and Zimbabwe, and in advocating for an end to apartheid in South Africa. In 2002, the OAU was replaced by the African Union (AU), which has continued to play a key role in promoting peace, security, and development in Africa, while also advancing the continent's interests on the global stage.

In Asia, regional organizations such as the Association of Southeast Asian Nations (ASEAN), established in 1967, have played a significant role in promoting regional stability, economic integration, and political cooperation. ASEAN's emphasis on non-interference, consensus-building, and peaceful resolution of disputes has helped to foster a sense of regional identity and unity among its member states. ASEAN has also sought to engage with other regional and global powers, playing a crucial role in shaping the geopolitical dynamics of the Asia-Pacific region.

In Latin America and the Caribbean, regional organizations such as the Organization of American States (OAS), the Caribbean Community (CARICOM), and the Union of South American Nations (UNASUR) have provided platforms for cooperation and coordination among countries in the region. These organizations have focused on issues such as economic integration, democratic governance, human rights, and regional security, reflecting the shared interests and aspirations of their member states.

The formation of regional alliances and groupings has been a critical aspect of the postcolonial experience, providing newly independent states with a means of building solidarity, promoting development, and asserting their influence in global affairs. These organizations have also played a key role in addressing regional conflicts, fostering dialogue, and promoting peace and stability.

Global Forums: Asserting Autonomy and Independence

Newly independent states have also sought to assert their autonomy and independence through participation in global forums and initiatives that promote South-South cooperation and solidarity. The Non-Aligned Movement (NAM), established in 1961, has been a particularly influential platform for countries seeking to maintain their independence from the Cold War rivalry between the United States and the Soviet Union. The NAM provided a forum for newly independent states to articulate their interests, promote disarmament and development, and advocate for a more just and equitable international order.

The Group of 77 (G77) and the China-Africa Cooperation Forum (FOCAC) are other examples of global forums that have played a significant role in promoting South-South cooperation and advancing the interests of developing countries. These forums have focused on issues such as trade, investment, development finance, technology transfer, and climate change, reflecting the shared concerns and priorities of the Global South.

Through their participation in these global forums, newly independent states have sought to challenge the dominance of the Global North in international relations and to promote a more inclusive and multipolar world order. These efforts have been particularly important in the context of ongoing struggles for autonomy and independence, as former colonies continue to assert their sovereignty and seek recognition of their rights on the global stage.

Ongoing Struggles for Autonomy and Independence: Palestine and Western Sahara

The Palestinian Quest for Statehood and Self-Determination

One of the most enduring and contentious struggles for autonomy and independence in the postcolonial era has been the Palestinian quest for statehood and self-determination. The Israeli-Palestinian conflict, rooted in the partition of Palestine and the creation of the state of Israel in 1948, has been a central issue in Middle Eastern politics and a major focus of international attention for decades.

The Palestinian people have long sought recognition of their right to self-determination and the establishment of an independent state. The conflict has been marked by a series of wars, uprisings, peace negotiations, and international interventions, with varying degrees of success and failure. The Oslo Accords of the 1990s, which established the framework for a two-state solution, raised hopes for a peaceful resolution, but the subsequent breakdown of negotiations, ongoing violence, and continued Israeli settlement expansion in the occupied territories have created significant obstacles to peace.

The Palestinian quest for statehood has also been shaped by the broader dynamics of decolonization and the global struggle for self-determination. Many countries in the Global South have expressed solidarity with the Palestinian cause, viewing it as a continuation of the anti-colonial struggle against foreign domination and occupation. The UN General Assembly has repeatedly affirmed the right of the Palestinian people to self-determination and statehood, and numerous international resolutions have called for an end to the Israeli occupation and the establishment of a sovereign Palestinian state.

The ongoing struggle for Palestinian independence remains a complex and deeply divisive issue in international relations, reflecting broader tensions between sovereignty, self-determination, and geopolitical interests. The conflict continues to pose significant challenges to regional stability and international peace, underscoring the difficulties of achieving a just and lasting resolution in a postcolonial world.

Western Sahara: Africa's Last Colony and the Quest for Independence

Western Sahara, a sparsely populated territory in North Africa, remains one of the last unresolved colonial issues on the continent. The territory was colonized by Spain in the late 19th century and was claimed by both Morocco and Mauritania following Spain's withdrawal in 1975. The indigenous Sahrawi people, led by the Polisario Front, launched a struggle for independence, declaring the establishment of the Sahrawi Arab Democratic Republic (SADR) in 1976.

The conflict over Western Sahara has been marked by a protracted war between Morocco and the Polisario Front, followed by a ceasefire brokered by the United Nations in 1991. The UN established the United Nations Mission for the Referendum in Western Sahara (MINURSO) to oversee a planned referendum on the status of the territory, but the referendum has yet to take place due to disagreements over voter eligibility and other issues.

The question of Western Sahara's status remains unresolved, with Morocco controlling much of the territory and the Polisario Front governing the refugee camps in neighboring Algeria. The conflict has been further complicated by regional rivalries, economic interests, and geopolitical considerations, making it a focal point of contention in North Africa.

The struggle for independence in Western Sahara reflects the broader challenges of decolonization and self-determination in the postcolonial world. The ongoing conflict underscores the difficulties of resolving territorial disputes, addressing historical grievances, and promoting peace and stability in a region marked by complex political, social, and economic dynamics.

The Rise of Emerging Economies from the Global South: Reshaping Global Power Dynamics

Economic Growth and Development: The Rise of the BRICS and Other Emerging Powers

One of the most significant impacts of decolonization on modern international relations has been the rise of emerging economies from the Global South, which have begun to reshape global power dynamics and challenge the dominance of the Global North. Countries such as China, India, Brazil, South Africa, and Indonesia have experienced rapid economic growth and development in recent decades, becoming major players in the global economy and international affairs.

The rise of the BRICS (Brazil, Russia, India, China, and South Africa) as a group of emerging economies has been particularly notable, reflecting the growing economic and political influence of these countries in global governance. The BRICS countries have sought to promote South-South cooperation, advocate for reforms in international financial institutions, and advance a more inclusive and multipolar world order. The establishment of the New Development Bank (NDB) by the BRICS countries in 2014 was a significant step in challenging the dominance of traditional Western-led financial institutions and promoting alternative models of development finance.

The rise of emerging economies has also been reflected in the growing influence of regional powers, such as Nigeria and Egypt in Africa, Indonesia in Southeast Asia, and Turkey in the Middle East.

These countries have begun to assert their influence in regional and global affairs, promoting their interests and seeking to shape the international agenda.

The economic growth and development of emerging economies from the Global South have had a profound impact on global power dynamics, challenging the traditional dominance of the Global North and contributing to a more multipolar world order. The rise of these countries has also created new opportunities for cooperation and competition, as they seek to navigate a complex and evolving international landscape.

Influence on Global Governance and International Institutions

The rise of emerging economies from the Global South has also influenced global governance and international institutions, as these countries seek greater representation, influence, and decision-making power in the international system. The demand for reforms in international organizations, such as the United Nations, the World Bank, and the International Monetary Fund (IMF), has been a central theme in the discourse of the Global South.

Emerging economies have called for a more equitable and inclusive international order that reflects the changing realities of global power. The push for reforms in the UN Security Council, where the permanent membership is dominated by the Global North, is a key example of the demand for greater representation and influence. The BRICS countries, along with other emerging powers, have advocated for a more democratic and transparent international system that better reflects the diversity and interests of the global community.

The influence of emerging economies has also been evident in global forums, such as the G20, where they have played a significant role in shaping the agenda on issues such as climate change, trade, and development finance. The inclusion of emerging economies in these forums has provided a platform for the Global South to articulate its interests and advocate for a more balanced and inclusive global order.

South-South Cooperation: Building New Partnerships and Alliances

South-South cooperation, the collaboration among developing countries to promote economic, social, and political development, has been a key feature of postcolonial international relations. Emerging economies from the Global South have been at the forefront of promoting South-South cooperation, building new partnerships and alliances that reflect their shared interests and aspirations.

Initiatives such as the China-Africa Cooperation Forum (FOCAC), the India-Africa Forum Summit, and the Brazil-Africa

Cooperation program have focused on promoting trade, investment, development finance, technology transfer, and capacity building. These initiatives have provided new opportunities for economic cooperation and development, reflecting the growing importance of South-South cooperation in the global economy.

South-South cooperation has also been evident in efforts to promote regional integration and development, such as the African Continental Free Trade Area (AfCFTA), the ASEAN Economic Community (AEC), and the Latin American Integration Association (ALADI). These regional initiatives have sought to promote economic integration, reduce trade barriers, and foster regional development, reflecting the shared goals of the Global South in achieving sustainable and inclusive growth.

The rise of emerging economies and the promotion of South-South cooperation have had a significant impact on global power dynamics, creating new opportunities for collaboration and competition, and contributing to a more diverse and multipolar world order.

Conclusion: Decolonization and the Future of International Relations

The impact of decolonization on modern international relations has been profound and far-reaching, reshaping the global order and introducing new voices, perspectives, and demands for justice, equality, and sovereignty. The participation of newly independent states in international organizations, regional alliances, and global forums has played a critical role in shaping global governance, promoting decolonization, and advancing the interests of the Global South.

Ongoing struggles for autonomy and independence, such as in Palestine and Western Sahara, continue to reflect the unfinished business of decolonization and the challenges of achieving self-determination in a complex and evolving international landscape. The rise of emerging economies from the Global South has further transformed global power dynamics, challenging the dominance of the Global North and contributing to a more multipolar world order.

As we continue to explore the broader story of decolonization and independence movements, the impact of these developments on modern international relations provides valuable insights into the complexities of sovereignty, governance, and development in a postcolonial world. The ongoing quest for a more just, equitable, and inclusive international order remains a central challenge for the global community, as we navigate the opportunities and challenges of a rapidly changing world.

Reflections on Decolonization and Independence Movements

Recapping the Journey: Struggles for Independence and the Global Quest for Freedom

The story of decolonization and independence movements is a profound narrative of human resilience, determination, and the relentless pursuit of self-determination and sovereignty. From the earliest uprisings against colonial domination to the formation of new nations and the subsequent struggles for political and economic stability, the journey of decolonization is marked by a series of transformative events that have shaped the modern world. As we conclude this exploration of decolonization and independence movements, it is crucial to reflect on the key themes discussed throughout this book and to consider their lasting impact on global politics, society, and international relations.

One of the central themes of this book has been the struggles for independence that unfolded across Asia, Africa, the Caribbean, and the Middle East. These movements were driven by a deep desire for freedom and self-rule, a rejection of foreign domination and exploitation, and a determination to reclaim cultural, political, and economic autonomy. The stories of these struggles are diverse and complex, reflecting the unique historical, social, and political contexts in which they occurred. From the Indian independence movement led by figures like Mahatma Gandhi and Jawaharlal Nehru, to the anti-apartheid struggle in South Africa championed by Nelson Mandela and the African National Congress, to the battle for sovereignty in Algeria under Ahmed Ben Bella and the National Liberation Front, each movement faced its own set of challenges and triumphs.

These struggles were not just about ending colonial rule; they were also about redefining national identities and reclaiming a sense of pride and dignity that had been eroded by centuries of oppression and exploitation. Decolonization was as much a cultural and psychological process as it was a political one, involving a profound reimagining of what it meant to be a free and sovereign nation in a world shaped by imperial legacies. Movements such as Negritude in Africa and the Caribbean Renaissance played a critical role in this cultural reawakening, challenging colonial narratives, celebrating indigenous cultures, and helping to shape new national identities.

The impact of these independence movements on global politics has been equally significant. Decolonization fundamentally altered the international landscape, leading to the emergence of dozens of new states and transforming the global order from a system dominated by a few colonial powers to one characterized by greater diversity and complexity. Newly independent states quickly asserted their influence on the world stage, participating in international organizations, forming regional alliances, and advocating for a more just and equitable international order. The Non-Aligned Movement, the Group of 77, and other forums provided platforms for these countries to articulate their interests, promote South-South cooperation, and challenge the dominance of the Global North.

The Legacies of Colonialism: Challenges and Continuities in Postcolonial States

While decolonization marked the end of formal colonial rule, the legacies of colonialism have continued to shape the political, social, and economic landscapes of postcolonial states. One of the most enduring legacies of colonialism has been the arbitrary borders drawn by colonial powers, which often disregarded ethnic, cultural, and historical boundaries and created artificial states with little sense of national unity or cohesion. These borders, along with the colonial strategy of divide-and-rule, sowed the seeds for internal conflicts and civil wars in many postcolonial states, as diverse groups struggled to coexist within the confines of newly established nation-states.

The stories of Nigeria, Sudan, and the Indian subcontinent, explored in this book, illustrate the complex challenges of nation-building in diverse societies marked by deep-seated ethnic, religious, and regional divisions. In Nigeria, the Biafran War highlighted the difficulties of achieving national unity in a multi-ethnic state shaped by colonial favoritism and competition for resources. In Sudan, decades of civil conflict between the north and the south, fueled by colonial-era divisions and grievances, underscored the challenges of creating a cohesive and inclusive national identity. In the Indian subcontinent, the partition of India and Pakistan, and the subsequent conflicts over Kashmir, reflected the enduring impact of colonial borders and the complexities of achieving stable governance in a region marked by religious and cultural diversity.

The legacy of economic dependency and underdevelopment has been another significant challenge for postcolonial states. Many newly independent countries inherited economies that were structured to serve colonial interests, characterized by a reliance on the export of primary commodities and a lack of diversified industrial bases. Efforts to achieve economic independence and sustainable development have often been hampered by these structural legacies, as well as by external pressures, including debt, structural adjustment programs, and global market forces. The experiences of countries like Ghana under Kwame Nkrumah, India under Jawaharlal Nehru, and Algeria under Ahmed Ben Bella, discussed in this book, illustrate the difficulties of transforming postcolonial economies and achieving inclusive and sustainable growth.

Despite these challenges, the resilience and determination of postcolonial nations and peoples in their quest for self-determination and sovereignty have been remarkable. Many countries have made significant progress in overcoming the legacies of colonialism, building strong institutions, fostering economic development, and promoting social justice. The rise of emerging economies from the Global South, such as China, India, Brazil, and South Africa, reflects the growing influence and agency of these countries in shaping global governance and international relations.

Lessons Learned from Decolonization and Their Relevance to Contemporary Issues

The history of decolonization and independence movements offers valuable lessons for understanding and addressing contemporary global challenges. One of the most important lessons is the importance of sovereignty and self-determination as fundamental principles of international relations. The struggles for independence were driven by a deep desire for freedom and self-rule, reflecting the universal aspiration for sovereignty and autonomy. In a world marked by ongoing struggles for self-determination, such as those in Palestine and Western Sahara, the lessons of decolonization remain highly relevant.

Decolonization also underscores the importance of justice, equality, and human rights in building a more just and inclusive international order. The newly independent states used their participation in international organizations, such as the United Nations, to advocate for decolonization, disarmament, economic justice, and human rights. Their efforts helped to shape global norms and principles related to sovereignty, human rights, and economic justice, providing a foundation for contemporary struggles for global justice and equality.

The experiences of decolonization also highlight the challenges of nation-building and governance in diverse societies. Many postcolonial states have faced significant challenges in building cohesive national identities and inclusive political systems that can accommodate diverse ethnic, religious, and cultural identities. The failures and successes of these states provide important lessons on the importance of inclusive governance, social justice, and reconciliation in achieving peace and stability in diverse societies.

The economic challenges faced by postcolonial states also offer important insights into the complexities of achieving sustainable development in a globalized world. The quest for economic independence and development has been a central challenge for many postcolonial states, reflecting the broader struggles of the Global South to achieve economic justice and equity in a global economic system shaped by historical inequalities. The experiences of postcolonial states in overcoming economic dependency, promoting diversification and industrialization, and fostering inclusive growth provide valuable lessons for contemporary efforts to promote sustainable development and reduce inequality.

A Call to Action: Engaging with the Histories of Decolonization to Address Modern Global Challenges

As we reflect on the stories of decolonization and independence movements, it is crucial to recognize that these histories are not just distant events of the past but are deeply relevant to contemporary global challenges. The legacies of colonialism continue to shape the political, social, and economic realities of many countries, and the struggles for self-determination, justice, and equality remain ongoing in various parts of the world.

For readers, engaging with the histories of decolonization is not only an intellectual exercise but also a call to action to better understand and address modern global challenges. The lessons learned from these historical movements can provide valuable insights into contemporary issues, such as global justice, development, and international relations, and can help us to build a more just, equitable, and inclusive world.

Understanding the complexities of decolonization can help us to recognize the importance of sovereignty, self-determination, and human rights in international relations and to support ongoing struggles for autonomy and independence. It can also help us to appreciate the challenges of nation-building and governance in diverse societies and to advocate for inclusive and democratic governance, social justice, and reconciliation in addressing contemporary conflicts.

Engaging with the histories of decolonization can also inspire us to challenge the legacies of colonialism and to promote a more just and equitable global order. The efforts of newly independent states to advocate for a New International Economic Order and to promote South-South cooperation provide valuable examples of how countries can work together to address global inequalities and promote sustainable development.

Finally, the resilience and determination of nations and peoples in their quest for self-determination and sovereignty serve as a powerful reminder of the enduring human spirit and the capacity for change. As we continue to confront the challenges of the 21st century, the stories of decolonization and independence movements can inspire us to strive for a world where justice, equality, and human dignity are respected and upheld for all.

The Ongoing Quest for Freedom and Justice

The journey of decolonization and independence movements is a testament to the resilience and determination of nations and peoples in their quest for freedom, justice, and self-determination. It is a story of struggle and sacrifice, triumph and tragedy, hope and resilience. As we conclude this exploration of decolonization, it is important to recognize that the quest for freedom and justice is an ongoing process, shaped by the legacies of the past and the challenges of the present.

The impact of decolonization on modern international relations has been profound, reshaping the global order and introducing new voices, perspectives, and demands for justice, equality, and sovereignty. The lessons learned from these historical movements remain highly relevant to contemporary issues, providing valuable insights into the complexities of sovereignty, governance, and development in a postcolonial world.

As we reflect on these histories, let us be inspired by the courage and resilience of those who fought for independence and self-determination and let us be motivated to engage with and learn from these histories to better understand and address the modern global challenges we face today. The quest for a more just, equitable, and inclusive world is a collective endeavor, and it is one that requires all of us to be informed, engaged, and committed to the principles of justice, equality, and human dignity.

Appendices

Glossary of Terms

- **Decolonization:** The process through which colonies gained independence from colonial powers, often involving political, social, and economic transformations. Decolonization occurred primarily in Asia, Africa, the Middle East, and the Caribbean during the 20th century.
- **Independence Movement:** A political and social movement aimed at gaining political independence and sovereignty from a colonial or imperial power. Independence movements often involve a combination of political activism, armed struggle, and diplomatic efforts.
- **Colonialism:** The policy or practice of acquiring and maintaining colonies or territories, often by force, to exploit their resources and benefit the colonial power. Colonialism typically involves political domination, economic exploitation, and cultural suppression.
- **Imperialism:** A policy of extending a country's power and influence through diplomacy, economic control, or military force. Imperialism often involves the domination of weaker countries by stronger ones for strategic, economic, or ideological reasons.
- **Self-Determination:** The principle that a people or nation has the right to determine its political status and pursue its economic, social, and cultural development without external interference. Self-determination is a core tenet of international law and decolonization.
- **Sovereignty:** The authority of a state to govern itself or another state. Sovereignty involves political independence

and the capacity to make decisions and enact laws within a defined territory.

- **Non-Aligned Movement (NAM):** A political and diplomatic movement founded in 1961 by countries that sought to remain independent of the Cold War rivalry between the United States and the Soviet Union. NAM promotes peace, sovereignty, and economic development among its members.

- **Pan-Africanism:** An ideological and political movement that seeks to unite African peoples and nations, both on the African continent and in the diaspora, to achieve political, economic, and cultural independence and solidarity.

- **Negritude:** A literary and cultural movement founded by African and Caribbean intellectuals in the 1930s that sought to reclaim African identity, culture, and dignity in response to colonial oppression and racism.

- **Partition:** The division of a territory or state into separate entities, often along ethnic, religious, or political lines. The partition of India in 1947 into India and Pakistan is a notable example.

- **Postcolonialism:** A field of study that examines the cultural, political, and economic legacies of colonialism and imperialism, focusing on the experiences of formerly colonized countries and peoples.

- **Cold War:** A period of geopolitical tension between the United States and the Soviet Union and their respective allies, from the end of World War II to the early 1990s. The Cold War influenced many decolonization processes and independence movements.

- **Economic Dependency:** A condition in which a country's economy relies heavily on a single or limited range of exports, making it vulnerable to external economic shocks and fluctuations in global market prices.

- **Guerrilla Warfare:** A form of irregular warfare in which small groups use tactics such as ambushes, sabotage, and raids against larger, traditional military forces. Guerrilla warfare was a common tactic in many independence struggles.
- **National Liberation Front (FLN):** A revolutionary political organization that led the struggle for Algerian independence from French colonial rule. The FLN became the ruling party in Algeria after independence in 1962.
- **Cultural Reawakening:** The process of reclaiming, revitalizing, and promoting indigenous cultures, languages, and traditions as part of the broader struggle for independence and self-determination.
- **Regional Alliances:** Organizations formed by countries within a geographic region to promote political, economic, and security cooperation. Examples include the African Union (AU) and the Association of Southeast Asian Nations (ASEAN).
- **South-South Cooperation:** Collaboration among developing countries to promote economic, social, and political development, often as an alternative to traditional North-South relations dominated by developed countries.
- **Zionism:** A nationalist movement advocating for the establishment and support of a Jewish state in the historic land of Israel. Zionism was a key factor in the establishment of the state of Israel in 1948.
- **New International Economic Order (NIEO):** A set of proposals made in the 1970s by developing countries to reform the global economic system to promote fairness, equity, and development. The NIEO sought to address the economic inequalities created by colonialism and imperialism.

Timeline of Major Independence Movements

Late 19th Century

- 1869-1884: Mahdist War in Sudan against Egyptian and British control.
- 1885: Berlin Conference leads to the "Scramble for Africa," intensifying European colonization.

Early 20th Century

- 1910: Union of South Africa gains nominal independence from Britain but under white minority rule.
- 1919: Egyptian Revolution leads to nominal independence from Britain in 1922.
- 1930: Salt March led by Mahatma Gandhi as part of the Indian independence movement.
- 1941: Atlantic Charter signed, encouraging self-determination and post-war decolonization.

1940s

- 1945: End of World War II accelerates decolonization; founding of the United Nations.
- 1947: India and Pakistan gain independence from Britain; partition leads to mass migration and violence.
- 1948: Israel declares independence, leading to the Arab-Israeli conflict.

1950s

- 1952: Mau Mau Uprising in Kenya against British colonial rule.
- 1954: Vietnamese victory at Dien Bien Phu ends French

colonial rule in Indochina.

- 1956: Sudan gains independence from Britain and Egypt; Suez Crisis marks the decline of British and French influence in the Middle East.
- 1957: Ghana becomes the first Sub-Saharan African country to gain independence from Britain under Kwame Nkrumah.

1960s

- 1960: "Year of Africa" sees 17 African countries gain independence.
- 1961: South Africa declares independence from Britain and implements apartheid.
- 1962: Algeria gains independence from France after a brutal war; Jamaica and Trinidad and Tobago gain independence from Britain.
- 1963: Kenya gains independence from Britain; establishment of the Organization of African Unity (OAU).

1970s

- 1971: Bangladesh gains independence from Pakistan after a bloody war.
- 1974-1975: Portuguese decolonization in Africa leads to independence for Angola, Mozambique, Guinea-Bissau, Cape Verde, and São Tomé and Príncipe.
- 1979: Iran undergoes a revolution, ending the Pahlavi monarchy and establishing an Islamic Republic.

1980s

- 1980: Zimbabwe gains independence from Britain after a protracted liberation struggle.
- 1983-1984: The Second Sudanese Civil War begins, rooted in colonial-era divisions.
- 1988: Myanmar (Burma) sees a major pro-democracy uprising against the military regime.

1990s

- 1990: Namibia gains independence from South Africa.
- 1991: Soviet Union collapses; many former Soviet republics gain independence.
- 1994: South Africa holds its first democratic elections, ending apartheid.

2000s

- 2002: East Timor (Timor-Leste) gains independence from Indonesia.
- 2005: Comprehensive Peace Agreement in Sudan ends the Second Civil War.

- 2008: Kosovo declares independence from Serbia.

2010s

- 2011: South Sudan gains independence from Sudan after a long civil war.
- 2016: Referendum in the United Kingdom leads to Brexit, reflecting ongoing debates over sovereignty and independence.

2020s

- Ongoing: Struggles for autonomy and independence continue in regions like Western Sahara, Palestine, and Catalonia.

Don't miss out!

Visit the website below and you can sign up to receive emails whenever Oswald D. B. publishes a new book. There's no charge and no obligation.

https://books2read.com/r/B-A-XWOIB-YPCZE

BOOKS 2 READ

Connecting independent readers to independent writers.